STONE
by STONE

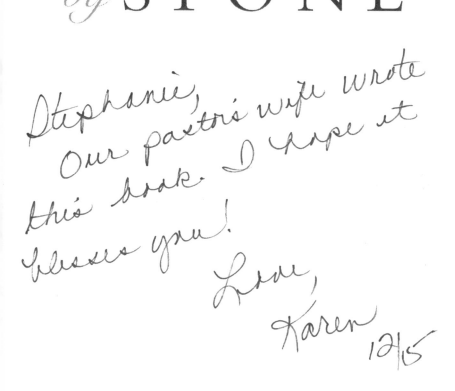

Stephanie,
Our pastor's wife wrote
this book. I hope it
blesses you!
Love,
Karen
12/5

STONE *by* STONE

Tear Down the Wall
Between God's Heart and Yours

JASONA BROWN

WhiteFire
Publishing

STONE BY STONE: TEAR DOWN THE WALL BETWEEN GOD'S HEART AND YOURS

WhiteFire Publishing
13607 Bedford Rd NE
Cumberland, MD 21502

ISBN: 978-1-939023-58-2 (digital)
           978-1-939023-57-5 (print)

To Doug
Not a page of Stone by Stone *exists without you.*

Table of Contents

Chapter One
A Boat, a Box, and a Girl Who Built a Wall

"Behold, I have engraved you on the palms of my hands;
your walls are continually before me."
~ Isaiah 49:16

"You will seek me and find me,
when you seek me with all your heart.
I will be found by you, declares the Lord."
~ Jeremiah 29:13-14

The Boat and the Box

The sea shimmered under the sun as the *Cape Hason*, my family's commercial fishing boat, chugged into the harbor of Tokeen, Alaska, in May of 1973. I was four and excited about docking, eager to run up and down on land, visit with fish-buyers and fuel-dock operators, and drink a cold orange soda—all impossible during the long, slow days we spent trolling for king salmon.

My dad slowed the boat to avoid making a wake, and the diesel engine rumbled deeper. He slowed it again and we were hardly moving. How could I speed this up? My dad would soon offload the salmon iced in the hold, down near the hull.

"Can I open the hatch, Dad?" I asked.

"No," he said. Then, "Well, I guess that's okay. Go ahead."

The wooden hatch—nautical grey—fit as a lid over an opening to the hold. I pulled it up, tugged it over, and shoved it aside while the boat sidled toward the dock.

My mom climbed out of the pilot house with a red handkerchief knotted over her black braids and grabbed a tie-up line. She stood with one leg over the rail, ready to leap off the boat and tie it to the faded wooden dock. My orange life-jacket pressed against my chest and scratched at the back of my neck.

Glancing down, I saw one of my shoes was untied. I couldn't run like that. I turned to sit and tie my shoe, and I sat in the open hatch. I fell backward, tumbling six feet to the bottom of the hold. The left side of my head crashed into the corner of the wooden box that covered the shaft, and I lay still against the cold wooden beams of the hull.

My dad threw the boat into neutral, leaving us drifting, and leapt down the hatch after me. As he lifted me up to my mom, the left side of my face drooped and my left arm hung awkwardly.

Tokeen, where less than fifteen people live year-round, is several days' travel by boat to a city with a hospital, and there were no phones to call for a plane. My parents relayed messages by CB radio, boat to boat, to reach the Coast Guard and ask for a sea-plane to come for me. Hours later in the hospital in Ketchikan, I cried as a nurse used scissors to cut my favorite striped T-shirt off my chest. And Dr. Wilson told my parents I had a depressed skull fracture; pieces of bone were cutting into my brain, disabling the left side of my body. No one at the hospital in Ketchikan could perform the surgery I needed to survive, and the airport was closed for the night.

But Dr. Wilson ferociously pursued help for me. He argued on the phone with administrators at Alaska Airlines, demanding they reroute and land the last commercial flight leaving Alaska that day, due to pass over Ketchikan en route from Anchorage to Seattle. Finally, he shouted that if they did not land the plane, he would lie in a field and shoot it down. They listened, and a commercial jet made an unscheduled landing to rescue me and fly me to Seattle for the surgery that saved my life.

How a Little Girl Builds a Big Wall

My mom brought me some old pictures a few years ago, and I looked for a long time at a shot of me taken in Seattle as I recovered from six hours of neurosurgery. I sit hunched in a bathtub, naked except for the white bandages wrapped around my head. The left side bulges. My lips are pressed together and turned up at the corners in a tentative smile. But while my mouth smiles, my eyes do not. Looking at the photo, I recognized in my four-year-old eyes the heavy fear that entered my heart that day. The enemy of my soul had begun his assault.

Trauma churns up our need to make meaning out of life: Why did this happen? What does this mean about me? About God?

Our enemy eagerly supplies his answers: lies. Jesus said when Satan lies "he speaks his native language" (John 8:44 NIV). The devil knows our wounds make us vulnerable, and he strikes just then. He wants us to absorb his lies so that we build a wall between God's heart and ours.

When I shattered my skull, my heart heard him hiss, "God will not protect you. He does not love you. You are not safe. This accident was your fault." God had rescued me, but I did not see it. I listened to my enemy. Accepting his lies, I cemented lie-stones into a wall between my heart and God's heart. They stood—preventing me from knowing the truth about God's love for me—for the next thirty years.

Two years after my accident, a friend invited me to Sunday school in Petersburg, Alaska. I remember walking alone through the rain and mud on dark winter Sundays to the wooden Baptist church at the edge of town. There among the felt boards in a classroom full of color, under the care of a smiling woman, I asked Jesus to come into my heart. I do not remember a day after that when I did not know Jesus was God's Son and the Bible was true.

But part of my heart stayed trapped—full of fear—behind the wall of lies. No matter how often I heard God loved me, I felt unlovable and unsafe.

Kids ran by me on the playground, knocking on the helmet I wore daily for six years as my skull healed. "Knock. Knock. Anybody home?" they taunted.

"You're ugly," the enemy told me. "No one will love you." I believed him.

Until I was thirteen I had an aunt—Nora—who sang, played the piano, and sewed life-sized dolls for me. And she had a little girl, Lauren. But when Nora was twenty-four and Lauren was four, my uncle John beat them to death with a steel rod from his weight-lifting set.

"See. God does not love you. Violence will destroy you or those you love," the enemy said. I didn't protest.

Each lie, like a malignant grain of sand in the soft flesh of an oyster, grew not into a pearl but into another stone. I had no idea I was blocking out the very love that would heal me. My wall grew as I cemented in other types of stones: anger at God, a mask, memories that would not heal, demonic oppression, and others. I will share with you more about them as we go on together.

So even as my commitment to God grew during my college years, my heart remained unable to experience his love. The stone wall kept it out. I knew my faith in God should make me unafraid, but it didn't. I feared brutal violence would strike me or people I loved and it would be my fault. I knew a Christian should be hopeful, but I wasn't. I dreaded that when I faced God at the end of my life, he would toss me out. I *knew* God loved me because the Bible said he did, but I *felt* unloved and abandoned. I despaired I could ever trust him enough, or serve him enough, to be someone he loved.

The Wall Comes Down

Then one night God helped me tear down some of the stones in this wall, and he engulfed my heart with his love. I shook with sobs and laughter. In astonishment and joy I understood God desired me, rejoiced over me, and treasured me.

I felt I had not—until that moment—understood the Christian life. I marveled that I could have been so obtuse. How could I have been a Christian for thirty-two years and not have comprehended the joyousness, immensity, and generosity of the love of God? How could my imagination have conjured him so meagerly? The wall between his heart and mine had stood in my heart all along, not his. He had waited, longing for me to tear it down.

I gasped with joy at a love "better than life" (Psalm 63:3). And I realized that martyrs gladly give their lives for Jesus, not because they are more committed, brave, or crazy than me, but because they know this love. Knowing it, they desire to be with God more than they want to keep their lives.

I understood how God could command me to love him with all my heart, soul, mind, and strength (Luke 10:27). How can I *not* love him this way, knowing the way he loves me? John's words, "We love because he first loved us" (1 John 4:19) rang true. The Christian life finally made sense.

I look forward to telling you more about this night in the chapter on anger at God.

Why This Book Is for You

I long for you to experience God's heart too. I pray this book will inspire and equip you to tear down—stone by stone—any wall standing between God's heart and yours. I hope you will flourish in the warmth of his passion for you. You have been looking for his love, whether you know it or not, all your life.

Picture a small plant rooted in the dirt. What does it need to grow? It needs soil and water, but it also needs exposure to the sun—a radioactive fireball so vast it could swallow 1.3 billion earths. Imagine if our plant were blocked from soaking up the gifts of the sun. We know it would wither. It might twist itself trying to find a scrap of artificial light, or its roots might go searching in dark places for some other source of nourishment for survival.

We are like this plant, except we require the sunlight of God's love. A little love from one source or another will not suffice. We need the *infinite* and *unending* love of the eternal God to make us sane, healthy, and free to become all God created us to be. If a wall of stones blocks the warmth of God's love from reaching us, we will not flourish. We might become twisted, and in our desperation we might search in dark places for what we need to live.

If you feel frustrated because no matter how often you hear that God loves you, your heart—impervious to what you hear—believes God looks upon you with disappointment or anger, I wrote *Stone by Stone* for you. I want to help you identify the stones preventing God's love from reaching your heart and to help you seek God to tear them down—stone by stone—until your heart celebrates, knowing your Father not only loves you but *delights* in you.

Each chapter in this book describes a different stone you might find in the wall between God's heart and yours and includes spiritual exercises to help you cooperate with God to remove that stone. Please spend as much time as you need with each exercise before moving on to the next. Some exercises may not touch anything for you, and you may move through them quickly. Others may require more time. Still others may call you to come back to them a month, or a year, or five years from now. I hope *Stone by Stone* will sit like a patient friend on your shelf, available to guide you whenever the Lord reveals a stone he wants to help you tear down.

You will also find at the end of each chapter a list of discussion questions to help you read *Stone by Stone* together with a friend, mentor, or small group. I pray you will have courage to seek at least one friend to journey through this book with you. God's love for you, shining in the eyes of another of his children, helps stones come down more quickly. And there is more power in praying with someone else than in praying alone (Matthew 18:20).

My Prayer for You

I pray any wall between God's heart and yours will come down, stone by stone. May your Father's love—an "everlasting love" (Jeremiah 31:3) that reaches as "high as the heavens are above the earth" (Psalm 103:11)—pour into your heart (Romans 5:5). I pray you will come to know more deeply the One who *is* love and be forever changed (1 John 4:16).

Spiritual Exercises for Chapter One

What Do I Long for in My Relationship with God?

1. Sometimes we are reluctant to admit our longings, even to ourselves, because we expect disappointment. Please ask God to help you become aware if reading this chapter has awakened in you any longing to know his love more deeply. Do you sense anything squelching that longing: Skepticism? Anxiety? Something else?

2. Prayerfully read Matthew 20:29-34. Jesus often asked people, "What do you want me to do for you?" Imagine Jesus asked you that question. What would you like him to do for you in regards to your relationship with the Father? Do you need help even hoping your relationship with him can grow? Please write your answer to him in a journal or notebook.

Do I Experience the Warmth of His Love?

1. Prayerfully read 1 John 4:16: "So we have come to know and to believe the love that God has for us. God is love." Ask the Holy Spirit to show you how you believe God feels about you—not how you know you are supposed to believe—but how your heart believes, regardless of what you know. Sit quietly for several minutes and pay attention to whatever he brings to your mind.

2. Please tell God what has come to mind and write down your thoughts, even if it's just a few words or phrases. Thank him if you have experienced his love. Express to him your desire to know more of his heart.

Do I Have a Wall in My Heart?

1. Isaiah 49:16 reads, "Your walls are continually before me." Most of us do not realize if we have a wall in our heart

blocking God's love. We think if there is a wall, it stands in *his* heart. Please ask the Lord to show you if there is a wall between him and you. Write down anything you become aware of.

2. If nothing has come to mind, please don't worry. You are inviting the Lord into the conversation with you, and though he is rarely predictable, he is always faithful. Be alert as you go through your days. He might show you something when you least expect it.

3. If you have ideas about what stones make up the wall between God's heart and yours, ask the Lord to help you tear them down, stone by stone. You may need to ask him for courage to do so. Consider making Moses's words your prayer, praying this every day while you read this book: "Satisfy [me] in the morning with your steadfast love, that I may rejoice and be glad all my days" (Psalm 90:14).

Discussion Questions for Chapter One:
A Boat, a Box, and a Girl Who Built a Wall

1. How do you relate to Jasona's story of struggling to know God's love for her?

2. Did reading this chapter awaken any longings in you to know God more deeply or cause you any apprehension?

3. Do you feel free to experience the fullness of God's love for you? Please explain.

4. What kind of wall might be standing between God's heart and your heart? Please explain.

Chapter Two
The Stone of a Dead Spirit
and Two Stones That May Conceal It

*"Do not marvel that I said to you, 'You must be
born again.'"*
~ John 3:7

*"And I will remove the heart of stone from your
flesh and give you a heart of flesh.
And I will put my Spirit within you."*
~ Ezekiel 36:26-27

One great and terrible stone stands in the wall between God's
heart and the heart of every person on earth. This stone must
come down before any other stone can be removed: the stone
of a dead spirit.

C.S. Lewis offers vibrant imagery for this topic in *The Lion,
the Witch, and the Wardrobe*. Four siblings stumble by magic
into Narnia. Edmund, the second eldest brother, succumbs to
the influence of the White Witch—the dreadful queen who
oppresses Narnia under a deathlike winter spell. Her offers
of power, delicacies, and special attentions dovetail with the
resentment he holds toward his brother and two sisters, and he
betrays them to her. With horror he discovers that rather than
elevating himself while putting them down, he has instead

played into the witch's hand and, according to the laws of Narnia, has given her authority to slaughter him.

Aslan, the lion-king of Narnia, takes Edmund's place. The sisters watch, aghast, as the witch and her hideous army humiliate and murder the magnificent lion. But just before dawn the magic table under his mutilated body cracks in two and Aslan leaps to life—larger, more powerful, and more beautiful than before. Winter begins to melt away from Narnia. Snow and ice drip into bubbling streams, and flowers bloom.

The children struggle to understand. Aslan teaches them about a magic, deeper than the magic of the witch, decreeing that the death of a willing innocent in the place of a traitor would destroy the table and cause death—all death—to work backward.[1]

Death working backward—this is what I am excited to talk to you about in this chapter. We'll start by taking a look at how things stand.

The State of the World and Our Place in It

God's good creation suffered a calamity—the fall. When Adam and Eve rebelled against God, death permeated creation. Now all creation "groans" (Romans 8:22) under decay, disease, and destruction. Things are not as God designed; we live in Narnia's unending winter.

As a result, when our mothers give us birth our bodies live, but our spirits—the part of us designed to relate to and unite with our heavenly Father—do not. It's as if we are born into the land where winter is the only season and Christmas never comes,[2] and inside our warm and wriggling bodies, our spirits—corresponding to the cold landscape—are dead as stone.

J.I. Packer describes this spiritual condition:

Sin is a universal, transcultural reality, an

infection from which no human being anywhere,
at any time, is exempt....it is also an energy, an
obsession, an allergic reaction to God's law, an
irrational anti-God syndrome in our spiritual
system that drives us to exalt ourselves and steels
our hearts against devotion and obedience to our
Maker. Pride, ingratitude, and self-gratification
are its basic expressions, leading sometimes
to antisocial behavior and always, even in the
nicest and most honorable people, to a lack of
love for God."[3]

With spirits dead in sin, we do not love God. We resist and
mistrust him. And while our spirits are dead, Christ does not live
in us. Without his life welling up inside us to knock down stones
between God's heart and ours, all other stones remain firmly
in place. So before anything else, death must work backward:
Our spirits must come to life. The stone of a dead spirit must
come down. How does this happen?

How Does a Dead Spirit Come to Life?

Jesus teaches that a person must be "born again" (John 3:1-8)
to enter his Father's kingdom. Just as we experience physical
birth, we must experience a spiritual coming to life—the Holy
Spirit making our spirits alive to God through Jesus. God
describes it this way through Ezekiel: "I will remove the heart
of stone from your flesh and give you a heart of flesh. And I
will put my Spirit within you" (Ezekiel 36:26-27).

Jesus reveals this mystery to Nicodemus, saying, "Truly,
truly, I say to you, unless one is born again he cannot see the
kingdom of God" (John 3:3). And Paul explains it in his letters
to the Colossians and the Ephesians:

*And you, who were dead in your trespasses and
the uncircumcision of your flesh, God made alive
together with him, having forgiven us all our
trespasses* (Colossians 2:13).

*And you were dead in the trespasses and sins in
which you once walked* (Ephesians 2:1-2).

*But God, being rich in mercy, because of the
great love with which he loved us, even when
we were dead in our trespasses, made us alive
together with Christ* (Ephesians 2:4-5).

God—in love—has mercy on us and stoops to blow his
Jesus-is-alive breath into *our* stone-cold, dead spirits. He raises
us from death to indestructible life in his Son. And in this way,
he tears down the stone of a dead spirit and rolls it away for
eternity. He works death backward. Only he can.

When God makes our spirits alive in his Son, they become
as they will be in eternity: "But he who is joined to the Lord
becomes one spirit with him" (1 Corinthians 6:17). Our spirits
live in Jesus, so when the Father regards us, he delights in the
beauty and glory he intended to display when he imagined us
into being. Our souls and bodies may remain wounded and
vulnerable to sin, but our spirits shine with the life of Jesus.
All further healing of our hearts—all tearing down of heart-
stones—flows from this healed place within us where our spirit
dances with the life of God's Son.

The Lord kindly gave me a picture of this once. I attended
a conference where Leanne Payne led us in an exercise called
walking through the garden of our soul.[4] She instructed us to ask
the Lord to lead us through our souls, showing us any "weeds"
of fear, unbelief, or sin growing there. I closed my eyes and saw
the wall of my garden, crumbling and in ill-repair; weeds of fear

grew through the cracks and tumbled over the broken places. I felt grief, but I wasn't surprised to see all this. I knew fear often choked my joy. But I glanced to my left, and gasped. There stood the loveliest tree. Sunlight spilled through its delicate leaves and the whole of it shimmered with life.

"Lord," I whispered, "what is that?"

"That is your spirit," my heart heard him say.

I was unfamiliar with the concept of the spirit, so I did not know what to make of this surprise. Much later, when I learned about our spirit being united with Christ when we are born again, I came to understand the picture. My soul was in shambles—no surprise—but my spirit was alive with the glory of Jesus. Surprise of all surprises!

The same is true for everyone the Lord raises to life in himself.

And the birth of our spirits heralds the beginning of the end of death's rule. For now, everything around us decays toward death. But spirits leaping to life are like the buds of spring announcing winter's end. Just as Aslan sprang to life and thawed the perpetual winter in Narnia, God, having raised Jesus to life, will make EVERYTHING on earth alive in a new way—no longer vulnerable to decay or death. Our living spirits glisten in evidence that he has begun this transformation.

Peter says, "We are waiting for new heavens and a new earth in which righteousness dwells" (2 Peter 3:13). And Isaiah describes what God has planned:

> *'For behold, I create new heavens and a new earth, and the former things shall not be remembered or come into mind. But be glad and rejoice forever in that which I create. ...The wolf and the lamb shall graze together; the lion shall eat straw like the ox, and dust shall be the serpent's food. They shall not hurt or destroy*

in all my holy mountain,' says the Lord (Isaiah 65:17-18, 25).

Paul says, "The last enemy to be destroyed is death" (1 Corinthians 15:26), and John says when this new creation comes to be, God will dwell with humankind and he "will wipe every tear from their eyes, and death shall be no more, neither shall there be mourning, nor crying, nor pain anymore, for the former things have passed away" (Revelation 21:4).

I like how John Piper explains it:

> God's purpose is that the entire creation be born again. That is, the whole universe will replace its futility and corruption and disease and degeneration and disasters with a whole new order—a new heaven and a new earth.... Paul...wants us to see that our new birth is a part of that.[5]

In the meantime, our living spirits unite us to Jesus's LIFE, just as branches draw life from a vine (John 15:5). And through that living vine, the Spirit of God grows his fruit in us: loving God and our neighbors; turning from sin; desiring to obey God; and trusting the cross of Jesus to cover our sins. His life in us fuels our desire to tear down the wall between God's heart and ours, *and* supplies the power of God inside us to help us tear it down, stone by stone.

How Do We Know If We Are Alive to God?

Jesus teaches Nicodemus that God's Spirit raising our spirits to life is mysterious: "The wind blows where it wishes, and you hear its sound, but you do not know where it comes from or where it goes. So it is with everyone who is born of the Spirit"

(John 3:8). God does it, and we don't know how. But Jesus also proclaims, "The kingdom of God is near. Repent and believe the good news!" (Mark 1:15 NIV).

So we have no control over our new birth, *and* Jesus calls us to repent and believe. God wants a response from us. Apart from repentance and faith we cannot determine whether a person's spirit has moved from death to life.

When Jesus asks us to repent, he asks us to turn away from sin *and* from trusting our own virtue. Born again people "wake up" to the reality of their sin, recognize its destructiveness and distastefulness, and strive to leave behind a sinful lifestyle in order to seek God (1 John 3:9). But people alive to God also see the futility of attempting to "be a good person" and earn right standing with him. Isaiah says our *righteous deeds* are "filthy rags" (Isaiah 64:6 NIV). A repentant person trusts only in Jesus's crucifixion to make him or her right with God. This is belief—faith.

When a person demonstrates repentance and faith, we have a pulse! We can celebrate the life of Jesus in that person. More fruit will come—most notably a growing love for God— confirming their spirit has indeed been made alive (Matthew 22:37).

Two Shadows that Can Hide the Stone of a Dead Spirit

Paul warns that we may think of ourselves as Christians and yet not be born again. "Examine yourselves," he says, "to see whether you are in the faith" (2 Corinthians 13:5). I want to help you do this if I can, because until your spirit is made alive with Christ's Spirit, the wall between God's heart and yours is immovable.

Jesus says eternal life is knowing God (John 17:3). He also says that on the last day we will face some hard surprises: "Not everyone who says to me, 'Lord, Lord,' will enter the kingdom of heaven.... And then will I declare to them, 'I never knew you; depart from me, you workers of lawlessness" (Matthew 7:21, 23).

Then he tells a parable about two men who did not know their father, the parable we call "The Prodigal Son." This parable reveals two shadows large enough to conceal the stone of a dead spirit: rebellion and self-sufficiency.

The younger son resents his father's authority and—heedless of the pain he will cause his father and of any danger to himself—grabs his half of the inheritance and rushes to squander it. This man characterizes the careless person who throws aside God's rule and lives for what he or she thinks will give them pleasure. He did not know his father's heart. If he had, he could not have chafed under the restrictions or requirements of such an adoring patriarch; he would have trusted that everything his father asked of him had to be for the good of his beloved son.

In our day, if this man thought himself a Christian, he might say on his way down the road with money jangling in his pockets, "I believe in Jesus, that's enough. I will live to please myself and surely it will work out. I will have happiness now, and in the end I will go to heaven."

Our fictional modern man fails to understand that his behavior exposes his unbelief. The Bible does not define belief as intellectual assent to truth—saying, "I believe in Jesus"—but as deep love for Jesus demonstrated by trusting obedience. Jesus says, "If you love me, you will keep my commandments" (John 14:15). When Jesus calls us to believe, he wants us to have confidence in our Father's goodness—as the younger son did not. Trusting God's goodness, we know obedience to him is good for us. The "fun" the younger son pursued led him to starvation in a pigsty. Jesus wants us to know rebellion leads to the humiliation and starvation of our souls, while obedience to God's commands leads to life.

A healthy born-again person does not live in premeditated rebellion. If we have sin we do not feel convicted about and have no intention to turn from, then we must take heed. Not only does our sin obstruct the healing we desire, but we cannot have assurance we are made alive to God. John says, "Whoever says, 'I know him,' but does not keep his commandments is a liar, and the truth is not in him" (1 John 2:4) and, "No one born of God makes a practice of sinning" (1 John 3:9).

Please do not think we need to question our salvation if we wrestle with sin. Our struggle indicates the presence of the Spirit of God in us because we do not like our sin. Paul expresses his own fight this way: "For I do not understand my own actions. For I do not do what I want, but I do the very thing I hate.... I have the desire to do what is right, but not the ability to carry it out" (Romans 7:15, 18). If the apostle struggled with sin, we certainly will.

I am also not talking about sins that erupt out of us without warning. These might be the kinds of sins James talks about when he says, "For we all stumble in many ways. And if anyone does not stumble in what he says, he is a perfect man, able also to bridle his whole body" (James 3:2). James implies that such a perfect man does not exist; we will each "stumble."

But to stumble, or struggle, while walking in the right direction differs from running headlong in the wrong direction. I am addressing those of us who have no intention of struggling against sin, but who rather intend to keep on sinning. If your heart is in this place, the things taught in this book will help you very little, because under the shadow of rebellion may lie the stone of a dead spirit. I plead with you to seek God to make your spirit alive if necessary so "Christ may dwell in your heart through faith" (Ephesians 3:17), and so his healing power can work through your soul.

So, the first shadow that may conceal the stone of a dead spirit is rebellion—a careless attitude that presumes on the forgiveness of God and rejects his gracious rule in favor of a sinful lifestyle.

The older son teaches about the second shadow: self-sufficiency.

This son stays with his father, enduring what he considers "slavery." Jesus tells this story in response to the Pharisees' disgust over his friendship with "sinners." The older brother is Jesus's portrait of these Pharisees, people who think their virtue puts God in their debt and thereby cut themselves off from God's heart even more severely than erring younger brothers.

After the younger brother returns home, the father throws a party, but he misses his older son at the celebration and goes searching for him. He finds the older brother seething in the shadows outside. The son accuses his father: "These many years I have served you, and I never disobeyed your command, yet you never gave me a young goat, that I might celebrate with my friends" (Luke 15:29). With this man, Jesus speaks to those of us tempted to think we have not sinned—"I never disobeyed your command"—and believe our service to God means he owes us something. Jesus warns if we persist in this thinking we will never know our Father's heart of mercy and compassion, and we will live behind a stone wall of self-righteousness so thick that his love will not penetrate. After all, at the end of the story, the younger brother celebrates, newly alive to the love of his father, while the older brother glowers outside.

So the second shadow that can hide a dead spirit or stifle the life of a newborn spirit is this kind of self-sufficiency, or self-righteousness. Today this person might be someone who does many religious things and trusts his "good life" to provide him entrance into the Father's kingdom. But, as we see in this parable, this person does not know the Father's heart either. The father remonstrates, "Son, you are always with me, and all that is mine is yours" (Luke 15:31). But the son remains unmoved. He has not stayed with his father out of love or gratitude. He does not see his father's heart of devotion toward him and his brother. He views his service to his father as slavery.

So in a person claiming to be a Christian, the stone of a dead spirit can hide in the shadow of careless sinning *or* obedience through gritted teeth. At the very least, self-sufficiency and rebellion are dark enough shadows to stifle our new life in Jesus.

The spiritual exercises at the end of this chapter will help you discern if either of these shadows hide the stone of a dead spirit in the wall between God's heart and yours. If you have not experienced the joyous healing of being made alive to God through Jesus, I long for you to seek him so he may raise you to life today, rolling away forever the stone of a dead spirit. May he unite your spirit with Jesus so you may repent of your sins, accept his forgiveness with joy and gratitude, and commit to loving obedience to him. Or if you are alive to God, but careless sinning or striving to be right with him on your own have over-shadowed and stifled your spirit, I pray you may receive grace to come out from the shadows and grow.

My Experience with This Stone

I believe I experienced new birth in Jesus when I was six years old in the Sunday school class in Petersburg, Alaska. I cannot remember not believing Jesus was God's Son and his death on the cross was the way to salvation. However, sometime before I turned ten, I was taught if I believed in Jesus I would go to heaven, but if I didn't believe in him I would go to hell. This frightened me for decades because I didn't know how much believing would save me. My performance-orientation bled into my spiritual life, and I needed to prove my belief by serving and obeying God. Only I could never do enough. I wondered if I moved to Africa as a missionary, slept on the ground, and ate only beans, would God accept me then?

I suffered from what Leanne Payne calls the "terrible passion to be perfect."[6] I tried not to sin at all and to hide the sinful side of my character from others and even from myself. Then I got married and had children, and the game was over.

A few years into my marriage, my husband Doug said to me, "You don't apologize for anything." His words pierced me. I recognized how admitting to wrongdoing terrified me because my internal rules dictated if I did anything bad—ever—then I *was* bad, evil, and unlovable. I believed if anyone had reason to be mad at me, then I was a terrible person and I had somehow tricked everyone who loved me. I could not accept myself as a beloved woman and also a sinner.

On top of that, I had never wanted anything as much as I wanted to love my children perfectly, but I could not. Before I had children I thought of myself as a person who never got angry. After children, I didn't even have to be fully awake to be angry. And who was I angry at? The dear little people I loved more than I loved myself. I saw my sin. Having a family helped me realize my twisted form of self-righteousness. I had been trying not to need Jesus's death for my sin and to earn my way into God's family—a terrifying endeavor.

I began to be more honest with myself, with God, and with others about my sin. I learned to sit with God, to *receive* his forgiveness when I confessed sin. I concentrated on apologizing—so frightening. But over and over, my husband forgave me; even my children forgave me.

Finally, my experience of God's love helped me step fully out of the shadow of the stone of self-sufficiency and accept that God has made me alive, that he forgives me and loves me, and that my growing love for him is evidence of the Holy Spirit living in me. I am humbled to realize I no longer fear he will reject me.

I long for you to have this confidence too. So wherever you find yourself today, I pray you will carefully pray through the following four spiritual exercises. I want you to experience new birth if you have not, or to come out from any shadow of reckless sin or painful self-sufficiency stifling your new birth.

Spiritual Exercises for Chapter Two

Do You Believe?

1. John 3:16 reads, "For God so loved the world, that he gave his only Son, that whoever believes in him should not perish but have eternal life." Please read through this verse thoughtfully several times. Ask the Lord to show you if you have any difficulty believing in God's loving nature, that Jesus is God's Son, or that Jesus's death will keep you from perishing and grant you eternal life. Journal anything that comes to mind.

2. If you have any such difficulties please ask God's Holy Spirit to come and help you in these areas. Consider how you could search out answers to your questions. These would be good things to talk to your mentor or small group leader about. Ask if there are passages of scripture they might recommend. Ask for suggestions on resources by Christian apologists which might assist you.

3. If you have no difficulties believing, please take a few moments now to praise God for giving you grace to believe. Consider what he has saved you from and worship and thank him that he has made you alive through Jesus Christ.

Where Are You in Relation to God?

1. Read the story of the prodigal son in Luke 15:11-32. Ask the Lord to help you find yourself in this story. Be open to his promptings, even if they surprise you. You may find yourself as the prodigal today, or perhaps you can remember being in such a place. Or you may find yourself relating to

the older brother whose self-sufficiency separated him more from his father than his younger brother's wildness could have. Perhaps you have never known the Father's heart of kindness and great love, and you must reconsider your image of God. Wherever you find yourself, pray to the Father from that place, pouring out your heart to him and asking him to help you return to his warm and loving embrace.

Are You Rebelling?

1. Read Romans 6:1-14. Ask the Lord to show you if you have chosen any premeditated, persistent sin. If he shows you something, ask the Holy Spirit to give you faith to repent of this sin and to be obedient. If you find yourself unable to give up this sin, please seek counsel and prayer from your mentor or small group leader.

Are You Striving to Be Perfect?

1. Read Philippians 3:4-9 and Isaiah 64:6. Ask the Lord to show you if you experience the temptation to trust in your own virtue, if for some reason you are frightened to bring your sin to Jesus. If you see this is true, please ask the Holy Spirit to give you the grace to repent of trusting your own works or good character. Ask him to search your heart and then confess any sin he brings to mind.

2. Now wait before him, allowing his forgiveness to soak into your heart. Make 1 John 1:9 your prayer of thanksgiving for forgiveness: "If we confess our sins, he is faithful and just to forgive us our sins and to cleanse us from all un-righteousness."

A Prayer to Come Alive to God through Jesus

1. If you have never "repented and believed" as I describe in this chapter, and you are ready to do so now, please pray the following prayer aloud:

    Heavenly Father, you created me and I owe my life to you. I have sinned against you by refusing to trust and love you and by choosing sin rather than obedience to you. I believe you sent your Son, Jesus, to die in my place—absorbing the punishment for my sin by suffering on the cross—to reconcile me to you. I long to be clean before you, to be close to you, to receive your love for me, and to love you in return. Please let Jesus's blood cover my sin so I can wear his righteousness and be your child. I repent of everything I know to be sin, and I acknowledge you are Lord of my life. I desire to obey you in all things. I pray you would give me power to cease my lifestyle of sin and to love you with all my heart, mind, soul and strength and to love my neighbor as myself (Matthew 22:37-39). I ask you to make my spirit alive to you through Jesus Christ. Thank you, Father, that you have heard my prayer and have had mercy on me. Thank you for loving me enough to provide this costly way for me to be saved. Help me to live for you and to allow you to live through me. Amen.

A Prayer of Affirmation of Faith

1. If you have confidence you have been born again, you may pray this prayer to re-affirm your allegiance to Jesus and

your trust in him:

> Holy and Triune God, I humble myself before
> you today to affirm my faith in you. Father in
> heaven, I praise you for being the creator of
> all things and my loving heavenly Father who
> has adopted me as your son/daughter. Jesus, I
> declare my faith that you are the Son of God,
> risen from the dead and alive forever. I declare
> my need for your forgiveness, and my trust in
> the righteousness you purchased for me on the
> cross. Please search my heart and show me if
> there is anything I need to confess or repent of
> today. *(Take a few moments of silence to pay
> attention to anything he might show you. Confess
> to him anything he reveals.)* I repent of these sins
> you have shown me. I declare you are Lord of
> my life and I desire to obey you in all things.
> I celebrate your promise that if I confess my
> sins, you are faithful and just to forgive me my
> sins and cleanse me from all unrighteousness (1
> John 1:9). Father, I ask you to fill me with your
> Holy Spirit to empower me to love you with all
> my heart, mind, soul, and strength and to love
> my neighbor as myself (Matthew 22:37-39).
> Help me to live for you and to allow you to live
> through me. Amen.

Discussion Questions for Chapter Two:
The Stone of a Dead Spirit

1. Was the teaching in this chapter about the birth of your spirit new to you or familiar? What are your thoughts about this concept?

2. Were you ever taught "believing in Jesus"—saying Jesus is God's Son—meant you were going to heaven? Were you comforted, frightened, or confused by this teaching? Please explain.

3. Do you now, or did you at another time, have difficulty believing the good news of John 3:16? If you overcame these difficulties, how did this happen? If you would like help overcoming any difficulties, do you have any idea where to search? Ask your friend, or your group, for suggestions.

4. How easy do you find it to trust that Jesus's death covers your sin? Do you relate to Jasona's story about her struggle with self-righteousness?

5. Who did you relate to—if anyone—in the story of the prodigal son?

Chapter Three
The Stone of Our Mask

"Grant, Lord, that I may know myself
that I may know Thee."
~ Augustine

"Behold, you delight in truth
in the inward being."
~ Psalm 51:6

"My people have committed two evils: they
have forsaken me, the fountain of living waters,
and hewed out cisterns for themselves, broken
cisterns that can hold no water."
~ Jeremiah 2:13

Our heart and God's heart can only meet in prayer when we bring forward our true heart—our real self. Though it sounds simple, relating to God—genuinely—proves difficult. To survive in this painful world, we wear masks to protect ourselves. And we don't just hide from everyone else behind our mask, we can fool ourselves with it.

This is why C. S. Lewis says, "The prayer preceding all prayers is, 'May it be the real I who speaks. May it be the real Thou that I speak to.'"[7] And this is why Augustine prayed for help knowing himself so he could know God. These men knew we tend, without God's help, to hide the truth about us and put forward a version of ourselves we hope God will find more acceptable—the way we do in almost all social situations—and that as long as we do this, we impede our relationship with God, our knowledge of him. Our mask stands as a stone in the wall obstructing our intimacy with God.

We can't fool God with our masks. Maybe we only sadden him. I know he waits for us to get real. He desires—even delights—as David says, in "truth in [our] inward being" (Psalm 51:6). He knows when we lower our masks, our relationship with him can grow. And he also knows our mask hides not only the less desirable parts of our personality, but also aspects of the person he had in mind when he created us.

With this chapter I hope to give you courage to begin removing this stone from your wall, lowering your mask with God, yourself, and others. Growth in our ability to receive God's love for us depends absolutely upon this kind of humility and vulnerability. My heart smiles knowing as you lower your mask, you will experience a great surprise—the warmth of God's love for you, astonishment and joy in receiving his grace, and loving acceptance from the people around you. On top of that, you will bless the rest of us, because God gives you—your real self united with him—as a gift from the King to his world.

The Crafting of a Mask

God dreamed up each of us in his great imagination before he made the world (Ephesians 1:4). Like snowflakes, flowers, and stars, he fashions each human being as a once-in-eternity work of art. And since men and women also reflect his image, each of us comprises a unique combination of his creativity, wisdom, courage, humor, skill, talent, and love—to reflect him as only we can. The person God had in mind when he wove us together is our real self, the person he will keep near him forever in his eternal kingdom.

But Adam and Eve opened the door of the human heart to sin and the door of creation to death, chaos, and evil. Now, when we are born, sin has already permeated and marred us. David says, "Surely I was sinful at birth, sinful from the time my mother conceived me" (Psalm 51:5 NIV). And threats of pain and rejection have saturated our fallen environment.

We know something is not right with us. And in this harsh world vulnerability feels like insanity. So like Adam and Eve who hid from God—jumping into the bushes to cover their disgrace and fear—we hide as well. We hide deep inside and put a mask forward to protect ourselves from what we most fear: rejection by God, others, and even ourselves.

We craft our protective covering by emphasizing and cultivating characteristics of ourselves we find more acceptable or that garner affirmation from those around us. We also stuff down less desirable parts of ourselves—both bad and good— and adopt traits that may be unnatural to our personality, but which seem necessary for survival. This remodeled version of ourselves becomes, as David Benner describes, the way we hope other people view us and the way we like to view ourselves.[8] It becomes our mask.

Since the Fall this inauthenticity feels necessary. Our enemy wants us to believe a powerful lie: If we lower our mask, rejection and mockery will destroy us. One of his chief strategies against us is the isolation our masks perpetuate. If we hide from one another, how will we learn that our struggles are the same? How can we offer each other tenderness and acceptance? How can we pray for and help one another? We can't. Satan has us where he wants us—alone in our fear and shame.

God calls us to a life of faith (Romans 1:17). We exercise faith in an important way by rejecting the lie that we need our masks, by lowering them, and by coming forward as we really are—deeply fallen and deeply loved. This kind of humility is the secret to life with God, the only path into deep communion with him.[9] And it is also the only route to authentic, rewarding, and healing relationships with our brothers and sisters.

Though hurt may abound, God promises nothing can ultimately harm us. Hebrews 13:6 says, "So we can confidently say, 'The Lord is my helper; I will not fear; what can man do to me?'" And Paul writes in Romans: "For I am sure that neither death nor life, nor angels nor rulers, nor things present nor things to come, nor powers, nor height nor depth, nor anything else in all creation, will be able to separate us from the love of God in Christ Jesus our Lord" (Romans 8:38-39). We do not have to be afraid. God delights in our truthfulness. He loves us. And because he is with us, no amount of rejection or scorn can harm us.

And think about Adam and Eve for a moment. There they were, hiding in the bushes. But before they sinned, they walked naked and unashamed before each other and God. Isn't it true that even after they sinned, God was not embarrassed by their nakedness? His perspective hadn't changed. He created their beautiful bodies and gave them glory (1 Corinthians 15:40). So hiding their sin, Adam and Eve also hid their glory. If we allow their story to speak more broadly, and move from the physical images to emotional ones, the same is true for us. Our masks may cover aspects of our sin, but they also cover parts of the image of God he intended to display through each one of us.

When God formed you and me, he designed us to be incomplete until we become one with him (1 Corinthians 6:17). When this happens, his life inside us shines with his beauty, his character, and his glory. Even our sin, submitted to him, grows us in gracious humility and increases our love for him and our gratitude for his mercy; we glorify him even in our fallen condition. But we can't become fully intimate in oneness with him while the stone of our mask stands between his heart and ours.

Our mask prevents true intimacy with God. When we hide

from him, presenting a cleaned up, altered, perhaps outright false version of ourselves to him, we stunt our relationship. Not wanting to face the truth about ourselves, we cut ourselves off from experiencing the depth of his love and acceptance, and we cannot become all that he created us to be.

My Experience with This Stone

In the first grade I liked to act as "project manager" on the playground, directing the other kids as we built dams in the muddy ditches. I felt strong.

But I remember at least one instance of someone shaming me for leadership. Playing on the beach with some friends, I was "in charge" again, when a man who knew me, but whom I didn't recognize, stepped out from behind a boulder. He had been eavesdropping on our play, and he said to me, in an eerily condemning voice, "That doesn't sound like the Jasona I know." He insinuated I had a nice and agreeable mask, but he had just seen my true self—bossy and overbearing. I got the message: My leadership was ugly and shameful. I had better stuff it down and put on the pleasant mask.

I distinctly remember refining this mask during my teens. I suffered through group projects at school, conflicted between my urge to take charge and my fear of being seen as pushy or bossy. I never allowed myself to show anger and trained myself to be compliant, soft, and inoffensive. Sometimes I couldn't muster an opinion—even when someone wanted me to—because I hid myself from even myself. *I* didn't know what I thought. To express anger or be seen as assertive would have toppled my self-image and filled me with shame. I also discovered my friends delighted when I accidently did absent-minded things, like wearing two different colored shoes to school or trying to back my car out of a parking spot before I started the engine. So I emphasized this part of my personality by making my foibles known and poking fun at myself. This lightweight image mitigated my peers' distain for my good grades, and they often called me an "airhead." I let it happen.

I had friends, but I didn't know myself, so no one could really know me. My relationships lacked depth, and I felt lonely. In college, I listened to others and not to my own heart and chose a major that did not align with my deepest passions or interests. And the first man I dated broke up with me because he couldn't be in a relationship with someone who refused to have opinions and desires. He would ask, "What do you want to do?"

I could only say, "I don't know. What do you want to do?" If I really did want to do something, I didn't admit it to myself.

I obstructed my relationship with God with my mask as well. I didn't dare to believe he could love the person I was inside. I thought he wanted me to be a super-human disciple. I expected perfection from myself. But I didn't know he loved me, so there was nothing to fuel my discipleship but will power, and I failed to live up to my standards all the time. My shame over failing increased my need to try harder and my fear that God was disappointed with me.

After college I didn't have the courage to tell my dad what I really wanted to do. So I went to a graduate school in Virginia because they paid my tuition. But as my mom and I drove across the country, I didn't even know which of their programs I wanted to choose. All I knew was that they offered Bible classes, and I wanted those for my electives. I hesitantly selected a degree in education during orientation. Then what was probably inevitable happened: At that school in Virginia, I chose a romantic relationship with a man whose insecurities tempted him toward controlling and emotionally abusive behaviors. Since I didn't know what I wanted or thought, he stepped in to tell me.

Six months later, I was a hollow shell. My parents caught on to the tenor of this relationship, and in light of what had happened to my aunt Nora, they did all they could to rescue me. My mom came out to drive me back across the country. Broken down, I finally admitted all I wanted to do was study the Bible, and my dad—who was not a believer—wrote a check for me to transfer to Regent College, a graduate school of theology. The grace and generosity my parents extended to me still brings tears to my eyes.

I had an image at the time of myself shattered and helpless as God wheeled me to Regent in a wheelbarrow. I hit the emotional bottom and knew I couldn't try any more to earn God's love. If he didn't love me already, I was lost.

I spent three years at Regent, and I found the beginnings of healing. There, I began to learn to drop my mask and come forward as my real self. Regent nurtures an authentic community, where people can be honest about their struggles and find acceptance, and where professors and students make transformation part of the everyday conversation. My professors drew out my real self by introducing me to a God of grace, by helping me understand my academic leanings, and by encouraging my love of literature and writing—parts of myself I had rejected and stuffed down.

And there I met Doug, the man I would marry. He was broken too, and our dating years were difficult, but I knew every week I spent with him I grew more whole. We have been married nineteen years now, and he continues to help me grow.

Doug's peers elected him captain of his high school football team, and at thirty-two he still projected that kind of leadership charisma. His handsome and muscular goods looks give him an appearance of confidence and strength. But I discovered he has the gentlest heart I have ever known, gentle down to the core. While we dated, he amazed me by *waiting*—every time—for me to tell him what I wanted and thought. He didn't run away, like my first boyfriend, and he didn't jump in and tell me like my second. He just waited. And he took seriously every single thing I let come out of my mouth: He listened to my advice, respected my opinions, and even taught me to fight with him. To this day, he doesn't act shocked or repulsed by my sin; he gives me grace and continues loving me. And he seeks out and affirms the woman he believes God created me to be, my true self.

When I was at my lowest, helpless to pretend any longer I could be a super-human disciple, God met me. He showed me kindness through my parents. And he sent me into a healing community and into a healing relationship to call out my true self: weaker and more sinful than I thought, but also stronger, more gifted—and more loved—than I had dared to believe.

Lowering Our Mask

Lowering our mask and learning to live as our authentic self does not happen in a flash. This stone comes down slowly over a lifetime. I still endeavor to allow God to do this more and more in me. We all need some things to help this process along: faith and humility leading to experiences of grace and love.

We need faith to believe—over and against the lie of our enemy—we can let down our mask and not die. Satan fiercely perpetuates this lie because the more honest we are, the more authentic and transparent, the more we draw people to us. Our authenticity invites theirs. My husband recently took a job at a new church where the former pastor, for twenty-four years, spoke with unguarded authenticity and transparency from the pulpit. People flocked to this church. His vulnerability made them feel welcome.

And our enemy knows as our mask comes down, God can get closer to our heart. He meets our truthfulness with grace, and our love for him explodes. He promises over and over to pour out grace on the humble (See James 4:6; 1 Peter 5:5; Proverbs 3:34). And Jesus promises, "Whoever exalts himself will be humbled, and whoever humbles himself will be exalted"

(Matthew 23:12). Our enemy wants so badly for us to swallow this lie because he knows the grace we will experience if we lower our mask; he knows our humility will allow God to transform us into powerful and joyful reflectors of his mercy.

Jesus tells the parable of the Pharisee and the tax collector to illustrate this reality (Luke 18:9-14). The Pharisee comes to the temple to pray: "Thank you that I am not like other men, extortioners, unjust, adulterers, or even like this tax collector." He tells God about his fasting and tithing. He presents to God a mask, sweeping his bad qualities aside to talk to God about his religious activities.

The tax collector enters the temple and brings God his sin: "God, be merciful to me, a sinner!" He acts on faith and brings forward his real self. Jesus ends the parable with this teaching: "I tell you, this man [the tax collector] went down to his house justified, rather than the other. For everyone who exalts himself will be humbled, but the one who humbles himself will be exalted" (Luke 18:14).

Jesus shows us the futility of attempting to get close to God by bringing him a cleaned-up version of ourselves. If we hide our sin and bring him a mask, we will never know the depth of his goodness, mercy, and love. We experience God's love more sweetly and deeply when we bring him our sin than when we do not; when we humbly confess, he responds with mercy.

Lowering our mask like the tax collector requires humility, a quality Jesus himself embodies:

[Jesus] though he was in the form of God, did not count equality with God a thing to be grasped, but emptied himself, by taking the form of a servant, being born in the likeness of men. And being found in human form, he humbled himself by becoming obedient to the point of death, even death on a cross (Philippians 2:6-8).

Andrew Murray lifts up humility as Jesus's defining characteristic, but he defines humility differently than we might expect. He says humility is not just contrition, but total and constant dependence upon God.[10]

So Jesus urges us to humility as well: "Whoever humbles himself like this child is the greatest in the kingdom of heaven" (Matthew 18:4). A young child has no mask. We know when children feel frightened, angry, happy, or hungry. We know when they want something another child has and when they need to go to sleep. And a child in good circumstances feels free and satisfied in his transparency and in his absolute dependency upon his caregivers. Jesus asks us to take the position of a child with our Father. Taking down our mask before God calls from us unguarded honesty about our sins, desires, griefs, and needs. And it calls us to utter dependence upon God: When we lay aside our mask, ceasing to turn to it to meet our needs and protect us, we turn to God to do those things for us. As he does, our heart delights in his tender and faithful care—his grace and love.

So we learn to drop our mask a little at a time. God is gentle with us. Jesus says, "I am gentle and lowly in heart, and you will find rest for your souls" (Matthew 11:29). One experience of vulnerable humility met with grace and love gives us courage to go deeper the next time, and further the next.

Peter's Mask

Peter learns more about God's grace and love *after* he denies Jesus.[11] When Jesus shares the last supper with his disciples, he tells them they will abandon him. Peter denies this: "Even though they all fall away, I will not.... If I must die with you, I will not deny you" (Mark 14:29, 31).

How does Peter see himself and Jesus at this moment? He views himself wearing the mask of one who will prove faithful to the death. And maybe he thinks of Jesus, "If I abandon him, he could not trust me to lead his followers."

If so, Peter is wrong—on both counts.

In the palace of the high priest, the religious leaders beat and spit upon Jesus during a trumped-up trial. People spot Peter loitering by a charcoal fire, identify him as one of Jesus's followers, and press him to admit it. Three times Peter denies knowing Jesus. The scene ends with Peter alone in the dark weeping "bitterly" (Matthew 26:75). Peter fails the One he loves at the worst moment; his mask is shattered.

This experience is excruciating for Peter, but now that he knows himself better, he will come to know Jesus more deeply. The resurrected Jesus finds Peter fishing and builds a charcoal fire, similar to the one where Peter's denials took place. Three times Jesus asks Peter, "Do you love me?" (John 21:15, 16, 17). Jesus uses Peter's former name, Simon, the word for "reed." (Peter—the name Jesus gave Peter earlier—means "rock.") Perhaps Jesus is telling Peter, "You are not a rock; you are a reed, swayed by the current. You didn't know yourself, but I know you."

Jesus serves Peter breakfast and gives him the opportunity to affirm his love for Jesus three times—the number of times Peter denied him. And wonder of wonders, Jesus assigns Peter the role of shepherd over Jesus's sheep, the same role he assigned him when he said, "You are Peter, and on this rock I will build my church" (Matthew 16:18)—long before Peter's denials.

Peter now knows he is not the unwaveringly faithful man he thought he was. His experiences the night of Jesus's death lowered his mask. But Peter also knows Jesus's love in a whole new way; more deeply than ever before, he knows Jesus loves him *in* his weakness and failure. The biblical writers never refer to Peter as Simon again. And they tell us how he leads the church in Jerusalem. Jesus's love—rich in mercy and compassion—transforms this fiery, mercurial fisherman from a reed to a rock.

Only by taking the risk of faith, by embracing the humility

Jesus calls us to, can we lower our mask to experience the depth of God's love for us, the love that changed Peter and will change us as well.

Idolatry and Our Mask

When we craft a mask, we come up with an image of ourselves we find acceptable and then we have to serve it. This means our mask functions as a form of idolatry, an idolatry of self. We rely on this version of ourselves, not God, to meet our basic needs. In this way, wearing a mask steers us toward depending upon ourselves and not upon God—the opposite direction from the humility Jesus calls us to. And a mask proves a cruel task master, demanding sacrifices while failing to reward us as we hope:

- If our mask requires success at work, we might sacrifice our marriages, our relationships with our children, and even our physical health to achieve career objectives.

- If our image demands physical attractiveness, we might push ourselves to be stronger, thinner, tanner, and younger-looking and despair over the natural decline of aging.

- If we think we must be helpful, we will never say no, though we seethe with resentment and fatigue.

- If our mask depends upon our possessions, consumer debt may rise, even while we lie awake at night, sick with anxiety over the bills.

- If our mask requires patience and kindness, we will smile while you provoke us, giving ourselves ulcers or cancer before we express how angry we feel.

The idol of our mask demands our service and many sacrifices, but does not reward us with contentment, peace, or joy. In fact, it distracts us from the pursuit of God. Our mask is akin to the broken well Jeremiah describes. We work and work, exhausting ourselves to keep our mask intact, but if the mask is a well from which we expect to draw life, we find it cannot hold water. Life leaks away. Meanwhile we miss the streams of living water Jesus promises to cause to flow within us (John 4:14).

Even on the human level, our mask does not give us the depth and satisfaction of relationships we think it will. It drives others away. When we approach others wearing a mask, they cannot know us, and we require falseness from them.

I read a novel with a character who had this problem. He cherished a completely wrong idea about himself. The author said he had "a favorite wrong idea about himself." The man believed he was generous, when in truth, he was stingy. To avoid the pain of admitting his greed, he spent his life trying to convince himself of his own generosity. He gave small amounts of money away and told people about his "acts of generosity." He wanted people to praise him, to be amazed at his benevolence. Others had difficulty relating to him because he needed them to affirm his false generosity and ignore his greed. People who would not cooperate were cut out of his life.

So our mask, crafted to protect us from abandonment, actually ensures people will keep their distance from us. Besides being turned off by the invitation to pretend with us, people will feel reluctant to be honest about themselves with us. Only with humility, warmth, and honesty do we encourage others to bring *their* real self to the table.

On top of this, when we make people "play along" by affirming our facade, deep down we know they are affirming a lie. In this way, the very experiences we seek to bolster us serve to reinforce our self-rejection.

This makes me think of Lance Armstrong's doping scandal. Armstrong won seven Tour de France titles and had the fame to go with such achievement. But he won those titles by using performance-enhancing drugs, and eventually they were stripped away. I suspect even before his exposure the fame and trophies didn't mean as much to Armstrong as they could have. *He* knew he cheated. *He* knew one day he might be found out. He lived behind a mask, a drug-enhanced mask. Trophy after trophy could not fill the gap he knew existed between the person he wanted everyone to think he was and the person he knew himself to be.

Armstrong's teammates finally cracked. Their grief and fear came out when they began to tell the truth. *Sports Illustrated* reported that investigators interviewing Postal riders had difficulty getting them to stop crying so they could speak.[12] Under the medals and acclaim, Armstrong's teammates felt guilty, scared, and lonely. No amount of winning could fill the painful chasm between their true self and their public mask.

Anything we gain through falsehood cannot satisfy. The mask may get us what we think we want, but it will never get us what our souls need—to be truly known and loved.

Lastly, and critically, our mask keeps our wounds hidden where they cannot heal. Bringing our hurts to light requires vulnerability. But when we hide our hurts, pretending they don't exist, they fester and do not heal. The recovery community wisely teaches, "We are only as sick as our secrets." Everything we keep in the dark has power over us. When we bring our secrets into the light, when we invite safe brothers and sisters into our true story, we break the power of shame. Bacteria multiply in dark, damp places but dry up in the sunshine. Our secrets are similar. James says, "Confess your sins to one another and pray for one another, that you may be healed" (James 5:16).

I belong to a group of volunteer prayer ministers who pray with those seeking emotional, spiritual, and physical healing.

Over and over I have seen people, with great trepidation, confess to a healing prayer team the sins and wounds they have never told anyone about. As the team regards them with steady love and acceptance, the power of shameful secrets evaporates and joy fills their hearts.

But keep in mind not everyone is safe. Please don't hear me urging you to indiscriminate vulnerability. To begin with, ask God to show you the safe people he has put into your life. Then begin to take risks with those people. I promise you will find blessing. Then, as you experience grace and love, you may grow so strong you can lower your mask with anyone, anywhere. But this is a process. Be patient and kind with yourself. God is.

Our True Self

The beauty of lowering our mask is coming more alive as our true self. Our masks resemble other masks, redundantly mimicking accepted ways of being, like middle-school girls who dress just alike. But God designed each true self uniquely—a once-in-eternity combination of gifts, preferences, passions, and creative ways of reflecting God's love and spreading his kingdom on earth. Your true self, united with Jesus, has something to share with the world only you and he can offer.

God births the potential to become this fully-alive-true-self in us when he makes us born again. Then, as we walk with God, growing more and more honest and humble, and looking to him in complete dependence, our mask comes down and our true self comes forward. As C. S. Lewis says, we don't find our true self by searching within ourselves for it, but by searching after God.[13] We look to God our Father, we depend upon him and do away with false ways of being, and he calls forward our true self.

I can think of twice when God did this overtly for me. During a time of painful self-doubt, I felt particularly frustrated with myself for what I saw as my lack of boldness. On top of that, someone had made a disparaging comment about the softness of my voice, considering it childlike, and this grieved me.

Then one night I went to an evening of extended worship. I cried out to God, "Why did you make me this way?" I didn't really expect an answer, so I felt astonished when I heard him say to my heart, "You are my anointing oil." The next day I searched the scriptures. I discovered people in biblical times used oil to commission someone for leadership, administer healing, and give gladness. Since I feel called to heal people's hearts, I delighted in these verses. Through them Jesus affirmed my softness and gentleness, saying he planned to use it in the healing of heart-wounds, like oil soothes and heals physical wounds. He called forward my true self. Since that time, hurting people have actually said to me that my voice soothed them when they were distressed. Thank you, Lord!

Toward the end of my years of staying at home full-time with my children, I didn't know my purpose. Several times during those months I sat quietly with the Lord, and he extended his hand to me—holding out a pencil. I didn't know what to do. I sensed him calling me to write, but I thought that had to be wrong. I didn't think I wrote well enough to write a book, and wouldn't Jesus want me to do something more service-oriented? As I told Doug about these experiences I realized with a laugh, "He has been handing me the pencil, but I haven't taken it from him!"

The next time I sat with the Lord in prayer, I took the pencil. Not too long after, the ideas and structure of this book came together.

I share these stories to encourage you to seek God to call out your true self, the person only he knows. And what he shows you may surprise and delight you.

May the Lord give you insight and courage as you seek him to lower your mask, to tear down the stone of mask-wearing. May he give you patience with yourself, because lowering your mask and becoming your true self is a life-long journey. And may you—the real you—the person God imagined in the depths of his great heart before the foundation of the world, come forth more and more to fulfill your unique purpose in the kingdom of God as he enfolds your vulnerable heart in his mercy and love.

Spiritual Exercises for Chapter Three

Please do not consider the following exercises one-time prayers. Hopefully you will practice confession to God and others, asking for forgiveness, honesty in your relationship with God, and seeking God to allow him to bring forward your true self as lifelong commitments to learning to live with your mask lowered.

Who am I, Father?

1. Prayerfully read Genesis 2:5-15, Psalm 139:1-18, and Ephesians 2:10.

2. Ask the Lord to show you how he sees you. Sit quietly and wait.

3. If you have questions about the way God made you, ask him.

4. Ask God to show you if anyone else's words have shaped you or tempted you to wear a mask.

5. Ask the Lord if there is something he would like you to do, something only you and he can do.

Why This Mask?

1. Prayerfully read Genesis 3:7-10. Ask God to help you to know yourself so that you may know him. Then put yourself in this story. Think of the fig-leaves as your mask. How are you tempted to put forward a version of yourself that is not quite the full truth? Do you know why? Record your thoughts.

2. Now imagine you hear God coming and you hide in the

bushes. God asks, "Where are you?" He seeks you. How do you feel about coming out of hiding? What are you afraid he might see? What do you fear others might see? Please tell God about these things, taking down your mask before him. Wait to see how he responds.

3. Ask him to help you to live more and more free from the need to wear a mask.

Confession to God

1. Read 1 John 1:5-10. Ask God to show you any ways you are tempted to say you have no sin. When he does, please take heart and confess that sin to him (come into the light) without rationalizing, explaining, or blaming someone else. Trust he knows all about it and loves you enough to die to free you from it. (Refer to the chapter on guilt and receiving forgiveness if you need help here.)

2. As you go through your day, you may experience small (or large) pangs of conviction from the Holy Spirit for a stray thought, a snide remark, a twinge of jealousy, or a fleeting delight in someone's difficulty or misfortune, etc. Do not ignore these messages from your conscience empowered by his Holy Spirit. Turn to the Lord and be honest. Confess to him and repent, asking him to change you. Do not evade confessing these sins to others when he gives you an opportunity.

Confession to Another Person

If you struggle with sin or shame, you can find a measure of healing and freedom simply by seeking safe people who will listen to your struggles or your story and pray for you.

1. Read James 5:16 and 1 John 1:5-10. Ask God who you can trust to hear your confession. Then ask him if there is anything he would like you to confess to this person so they may pray for you.

2. Contact this person and find a time for them to listen to you. Please don't forget to ask them to pray for you before you part. If this exercise is difficult for you, you may start small. Remember, each time you lower your mask and experience grace, you will gain the courage to go a little deeper the next time.

The Discipline of Asking for Forgiveness

1. Read Matthew 5:23-24. Ask the Lord to show you if there is anyone from whom you need to seek forgiveness. Ask him to grace you with humility and courage so you can confess your sin to this person and ask them to forgive you. Purpose to have this conversation as soon as possible. When you do, resist the temptation to defend yourself, offer excuses, or tell them how they caused you to sin. Simply be honest about your sin and humbly ask for forgiveness.

Honesty about Our Heart

1. We also hide our true selves behind a mask by burying parts of ourselves that are not sinful. Read 1 Samuel 1:15-16 and Psalm 62:8. Be honest with God about your desires, dreams, sorrows, disappointments, hopes, and joys. Pour out your heart to him. Is there something creative or heroic you have longed to do but felt disqualified from pursuing? Tell him about this.

Discussion Questions for Chapter Three:
The Stone of Our Mask

1. Had you ever considered how we tend to wear a mask when we pray? What are your thoughts about this after reading this chapter?

2. Who has been the most authentic, transparent person you have known? How did you feel around this person?

3. Talk a little about why Andrew Murray would consider humility Jesus's primary characteristic. What are your thoughts about this?

4. Do you have a community or relationship that invites transparency, where you can be safe being honest? How can you offer this kind of community to others?

5. Jasona talked about hiding both anger and leadership. What sins or character traits do you think men are most likely to hide? How about women?

6. Jasona also talked about taking wrong turns in her life because she did not know herself. How do you relate, or not, to her story?

7. Do you have dreams about things you would like to do in God's kingdom? Have you suppressed or dismissed them? Why?

Chapter Four
The Stone of Lies

"You will know the truth, and the truth will set you free."
~ John 8:32

*"When he lies, he speaks his native language,
for he is a liar and the father of lies."*
~ John 8:44 NIV

*"The sin underneath all our sins is to trust the lie of the
serpent that we cannot trust the love and grace of Christ
and must take matters into our own hands."*
~ Martin Luther

Truth, Lies, and Choices

Adam and Eve heard the truth, followed by a lie. Then they made a choice.

God told them they could eat the fruit of any tree in the garden except the tree of the knowledge of good and evil, "for in the day that you eat of it you shall surely die" (Genesis 2:17).

Satan hissed to Eve, "You will not surely die. For God knows that when you eat of it your eyes will be opened, and you will be like God" (Genesis 3:4-5). He disparaged God's goodness, insinuating, "God has deceived you. He's holding out on you. You are a fool if you trust what he says." And he tempted her with fruit that was a "delight to the eyes" and desirable to "make one wise" (Genesis 3:6).

The first man and woman chose to believe the lie: "Yes," they said, "God is not trustworthy. He is keeping something good from us." They ate the fruit, severing their intimacy with their heavenly Father. The terrible separation spawned death on all levels—natural disaster, disease, bereavement, violence, and war—as God warned it would.

And every human since—with the exception of One—has heard the enemy lie, believed him to some degree, and suffered separation from God's heart as those lies solidified into stones in the wall between God's heart and theirs.

But that One...

Perhaps no one has been tested more severely than Jesus. After his baptism, Jesus went into the desert and fasted for forty days and nights. Satan found him starving and parched, both of them knowing Jesus's obedience to his Father would lead him to the cross.

In Matthew 4:1-11, Satan offered tempting solutions to Jesus's difficulties, laced with insinuated lies about the Father: "Turn rocks into bread" (Meet your needs yourself; your Father has abandoned you.); "Throw yourself down from the temple so everyone will see the angels save you" (Prove your identity the easy way; the cross isn't necessary.); and "I will give you all the kingdoms of the world and their glory" (Seize pleasure and power; your Father is denying you, leaving you in poverty and obscurity.).

Twice during this battle, Satan sneered the most awful insinuation of all: "If you are the Son of God…" (Matthew 4:3, 6). *If* you are the Son? God had just said to Jesus, and to all within hearing as Jesus rose dripping from his baptism, "This is my beloved Son, with whom I am well pleased" (Matthew 3:17).

But Satan's temptations and lies tore at God's affirmation: "Either you aren't his son," he implied, or "he is a cruel father, to leave you like this. And we know where his cruelty will take you. I have another way."

Tested in a wilderness as opposed to a garden, Jesus chose differently than Adam and Eve. He rejected the lies of the enemy, no matter how his suffering seemed to belie his identity as God's beloved. He believed his Father's words. *He entrusted himself to the goodness of his Father*. And his trusting obedience rescued and restored the dying human race.

But until Jesus returns, Satan and his workers continue to lie, maligning God's heart. They find us in our weakest moments and whisper their hideous insinuations. We must choose: agree with him, like Adam and Eve, and open the door for his dark plans—or resist him, like Jesus, and open the door for the kingdom of God.

In this chapter, I am going to ask you to consider what lies our enemy has told you and the choices you made when he did. More than that, I am going to ask you to reflect on the ways your heavenly Father has spoken the truth to you. I want to help you choose to believe him. The spiritual exercises at the end of this chapter will ask you to look at the story of your life to separate the lies of the enemy from the truth of God. They will help you identify lie-stones in the wall between God's heart and yours and help you seek God to tear them down.

It gives me joy to tell you if you have believed the lies of your enemy like I did, Jesus—who came "to destroy the works of the devil" (1 John 3:8)—can help you tear down those lies, stone by stone. He will plant truth in their place, the truth about God's good heart and his regard for you as his beloved, the truth Jesus believed.

Your Story: Truth and Lies

In the stories of Adam and Eve and Jesus, we can see how the heavenly Father told them the truth and the enemy tempted them to believe lies. In my story the same things happened: 1) the enemy lied; and 2) the Father told the truth.

In the first chapter I told you some of the lies my adversary whispered to me: "God will not keep you safe. Your accident was your fault. You are unlovable." I didn't realize I was doing it, but I believed my enemy about these things. My acquiescence cemented these lie-stones into the wall standing between God's heart of love and my own wounded heart, keeping me in the shadows of fear and loneliness.

But God was also telling me the truth. He used words, circumstances, and creation to tell me a different story than the one my enemy wanted me to believe. He rescued me when I was hurt, putting Dr. Wilson in my path to fight for an airplane for me. He sent a faithful woman to invite me to Sunday school where I would hear about him and be encouraged to invite him into my heart. Later, he sent Young Life leaders to befriend me and an Intervarsity Christian Fellowship worker to come alongside me and start a Bible study in my dorm. He made sure I had a Bible. He also captivated my heart with the beauty of his creation: I delighted to watch waves roll, northern lights dance, and dolphins leap; I loved racing across an open field bareback on my horse and then resting on her warm back in the sun while she munched dry grass; I marveled that he would create anything so charming as our cocker spaniel puppy. In all these ways God was telling me he is good and he loves me. I just had a hard time believing him.

Most of us have considered, at least a little, how God has told us the truth. We may be able to describe how he drew us to himself through certain circumstances. But I encourage you to think some more about the ways God has told you the truth. We do live in a fallen world, under the influence of our enemy. But our heavenly Father continues to provide good things all over creation and in every human life. He holds all of creation together (Colossians 1:17) and the beauty and goodness of created things proclaim his presence and faithfulness (Psalm 19:1). Every good thing you have seen or experienced—the love of your family or a friend, the colors of a sunset, the shimmer of snow, a job or hobby that fills you with satisfaction, the glory of flowers in bloom—every single, good thing is evidence of God's continued care for his creation and for you.

I pray you can agree in spite of how terrible things might have been for you at times—or in spite of how much pain you may be in today—God's goodness has touched your life. Hell is the place where God's goodness is absent, but both goodness and evil touch us here on earth.

And we look forward to heaven where God's goodness and beauty prevail eternally. I know a little boy who dreamed Jesus took him to heaven. He woke with his face radiating joy. When his parents asked him what heaven was like, he said, "There wasn't a single badness anywhere."

Yes. Not a single badness. In heaven, there will be no "mourning, nor crying, nor pain anymore" (Revelation 21:4). We long for that place, but we live in this one, our stories riddled with joy and sorrow, pain and solace.

So as you consider the story of your life and think about the ways God has told you the truth, ponder a little more deeply than you may have done before. What good things have filled you with joy? Has God spoken to you about himself through these gifts?

The other side of your story tells of the assaults and lies of the evil one, and the falsehoods you believed. Most of us have not considered how our enemy has schemed against us to trap us in lies, but you will have that opportunity now.

Laurie's story illustrates what I am asking you to think about. Today Laurie is a married mother of a delightful brood. But when she was young she was sexually abused by an older girl. And the enemy lied to her: "This is your fault. You must be a lesbian." When Laurie grew older, someone made a comment about her being gay that confused and hurt her. Then a college girlfriend tried to kiss her. The enemy kept up his lies. He wanted her to believe she was a lesbian, so he used these assaults as part of his scheme to convince Laurie her sexuality was disordered.

When the enemy attacks us over and over in a thematic way, we grow increasingly vulnerable to accepting his lies about our experiences. The violence in my family made it easy for him to tell me God is distant and I am not worthy of love and protection. Laurie's painful experiences gave him the opportunity to lie to her about her sexual orientation. Experience doesn't lie, or so we think. But I ask you to consider that it can, and does, when it is manipulated and interpreted by our enemy.

Help for This Chapter's Spiritual Exercises

Looking for Truth and Lies

You have lived a unique story, but I do not doubt you will see these two streams in your life as you take the time to look: the Father telling you the truth with love and the enemy scheming to trap you in lies. I pray you will discover any lies that have hardened into stones in your heart. I also pray you will feel joy and gratitude as you see the ways God has sought you and shown himself to you so you can know the truth of his love for you.

Watching for Questions Your Heart Asks

As you work through these exercises, notice any questions coming up from your heart. You might find yourself asking, "Why did God let this happen to me?" or "What is wrong with me?" I know these questions hurt, but please don't push them away. Write them down as the honest cries of your heart. These questions can work like important clues, helping you discover lie-stones. They arise from your need to make meaning of life. If they come up, this isn't the first time your heart has asked them, and the enemy may have planted lies in response to them.

You will need as many clues as possible because lies are

difficult to uncover. If we have accepted a lie, it doesn't seem like a lie to us. It feels like truth. The Holy Spirit must do a work in us just to help us *suspect* that something we believe is not the truth, but a lie instead. I pray he will begin this work in you through this chapter.

Sharing Your Story

In the discussion questions for this chapter, I ask you to share your story with your small group, mentor, spouse, or trusted friend. I ask you to take this risk because bringing others into this process will expedite your healing. God uses the hearts and ears of people who love us to mediate his love to us. Sitting with someone while they listen with compassion to the story of your life and reflect love and acceptance to you can bring a measure of healing.

Patience with Yourself

This chapter only begins the process outlined in this book. If you uncover any lies, I provide a simple prayer exercise to help you allow Jesus to remove lie-stones and replace them with truth. But other things may stand in the way. As you will learn, the lie-stones in my own heart did not come down until the stone of anger at God came down first. So if you do not get relief immediately, don't worry. We will come at these issues in many other ways before the end of the book. You may even uncover lies at different points and return to jot them into your story or pray again through these spiritual exercises. Please do not demand from yourself a linear, one-time process.

May God bless you as you pray through the story of your life. I pray he will show you more of his great love for you as you see his initiatives toward you more clearly. And may he give you discernment to recognize the lies your enemy has planted in your heart to malign God's character and make you doubt your worthiness to be loved by him. May these lie-stones come down.

Spiritual Exercises for Chapter Four

As these spiritual exercises ask you to think through the story of your life, please write it out, either on a timeline, in prose, in the form of columns, or any way natural for you. Consider using two different colored pens—one for the ways God told you the truth, and another for the attacks and lies of your enemy. Please take as much time as you need to create this timeline—several days or even a couple of weeks might be best.

Your Life from Birth to Age Ten

1. Prayerfully read Psalm 139:1-18.

2. Ask the Holy Spirit to help you discern the ways your Father told you the truth and your enemy told you lies.

3. Think about and record your life from birth to age ten. Consider any special circumstances surrounding your conception or the time you spent in your mother's womb. Record any vivid memories, positive or negative, of your early childhood. Think of ways the Lord demonstrated or told you of his love. Did you experience delight in creation, in music, in play? Were there any people who made you feel special and loved or who told you about God's goodness? Did the Lord ever rescue you? See if you can discern any ways the enemy tried to destroy you or lie to you during those early years.

4. Respond to God about what you have seen. You might want to thank him, to ask him painful questions, or even to confess to him that you are angry with him.

Your Life from Age Ten to Twenty

1. Prayerfully read Psalm 18:1-19.

2. Ask the Holy Spirit to help you see what God was doing in your life during these years and any ways the enemy came against you and lied to you.

3. Think about and record your story from age 10 to 20. These questions might help you get started:

    *   Who or what shaped your self-understanding during this time?

    *   How was your emerging sexuality exploited, shamed, or nurtured during these years?

    *   Did God rescue you from anything during these years?

    *   Can you begin to see a theme to the enemy's attacks?

    *   Do you recognize any lies you believed about God or about yourself?

4. Respond to God in prayer about what you have discerned.

Your Life from Age Twenty to the Present

1. Prayerfully read 2 Corinthians 1:8-11.

2. Again, ask the Holy Spirit to help you discern both God's truth and Satan's lies in your story.

3. Now work through your story, decade by decade, until you reach the present time. These questions might help you:

    *   Did you marry? Did you not marry?

    *   What blessings have come to you in marriage or in singleness? What heartbreaks?

- What lies might you have believed through these experiences?

- What has your employment experience been like?

- Did you discover who God made you to be or did you feel overlooked and insignificant?

- If you became a parent or did not have children, consider how these experiences have shaped your understanding of God and of yourself.

- Were there lies the enemy planted in your childhood that seemed to come true through your adult years?

- How have your struggles helped you to "rely on God"?

4. Spend some time responding to God in prayer about what you have recorded.

Four: Replace a Lie with God's Truth through Prayer

1. Prayerfully read John 14:6 and John 8:31-32.

2. Confess to Jesus the specific lie you have believed and ask him to tell you or show you the truth he wants to take the place of that lie in your heart. You may pray something like this:

> "Lord Jesus, Lord of all creation (Colossians 1:16), I praise you for being the way, the truth, and the life (John14:6), for speaking only truth (Isaiah 45:19). I trust your truth, when I believe it in my deepest heart, will set me free (John 8:32). I confess to you I have believed the lie that _____. I repent before you for having traded your truth for this lie

(Romans 1:25). I want this lie to have no more power to shape or influence me. I long for your truth to fill all the places in me occupied by this lie, and I renounce this lie from my enemy in the name of my Lord, Jesus Christ. I ask you now, Lord, to speak or to show me the truth you want me to receive in place of this lie."

(Wait upon the Lord in silence, attentive to anything you hear him say, or anything he shows you. If you receive anything from him, sit quietly with him, letting it soak into your heart. Finally, if the Lord has shown or spoken to you any truth, write it down.)

3. If the Lord has replaced any lies with his truth, thank him from your heart, and pray something like this:

   "Lord, I thank you for the truth you have ministered to me today. I receive it from you with gratitude, and I desire to walk in this truth from this day forward. I ask for your help to do this, and I pray you protect me from any lies the enemy would tell me to steal this truth from me. I pray as the man in Mark 9:24 did so long ago, 'I believe; help my unbelief!'"

4. If you are unable to hear from the Lord or experience the removal of this lie from your heart, please don't be discouraged. Even the ability to recognize something as a lie is a tremendous work of the Holy Spirit. And as I said at the end of this chapter, we are only beginning this process. The lie you are fighting may be held in place by other stones. Simply ask the Lord over the days and weeks to continue to free you from this lie.

Discussion Questions for Chapter Four:
The Stone of Lies

1. Please take time to share your story with your small group, mentor, spouse, or trusted friend. Ask whoever listens to you to help you discern any additional lies that have shaped you and blocked you from God's love.

2. What thoughts or feelings did you have toward Jesus as you considered his battle against the enemy?

3. Had you ever considered the ways God has told you the truth through the story of your life? What was this experience like for you?

4. Had you ever considered the ways the enemy has schemed against you through your life? If not, what was this experience like for you?

5. What did you learn about yourself, about God, or about the enemy through this chapter?

6. If you received some insight about lies you may have believed, please talk about this.

7. Share your experience of seeking Jesus to remove lie-stones and replace them with truth.

Chapter Five
The Stone of Guilt

*"We may plead for mercy for a lifetime in
unbelief, and at the end of our days be still
no more than sadly hopeful that we shall
somewhere, sometime, receive it. This is to
starve to death just outside the banquet hall in
which we have been warmly invited."*
~ A.W. Tozer.[14]

*"The steadfast love of the Lord never ceases;
his mercies never come to an end;
they are new every morning"*
~ Lamentations 3:22-23

When a stone of guilt divides our heart from God's heart,
we may believe God forgives others, but we cannot trust
his forgiveness for ourselves. We identify ourselves by the
cross—God's forgiveness—yet we live guilt-ridden, anxious,
and fatigued by our efforts to be good enough for him. God's
mercy seems too good to be true.

The stone of guilt also causes a painful fracture between
our mind and our deepest self. Our mind understands God's
forgiveness, but our heart—kept from the joy of receiving
forgiveness—withers in guilt. From what I can tell, more
Christians live this way than do not.

C.S. Lewis experienced this problem, but one day the stone

rolled away, and God's forgiveness reached his heart. He described his experience in a letter to a friend:

> Everything without, and many things within, are marvellously well at present. Indeed...I realise that until about a month ago I never really believed (tho' I thought I did) in God's forgiveness. What an ass I have been both for not knowing and for thinking I knew. I now feel that one must never say one believes or understands anything: any morning a doctrine I thought I already possessed may blossom into this new reality.[15]

Psalm 34:8 invites us to "Taste and see that the Lord is good!" Jonathan Edwards says the difference between *knowing* God is forgiving and *experiencing* his forgiveness is like the difference between believing honey is sweet versus tasting honey on our tongue.[16]

If you feel guilty—if you have pleaded with God to forgive you but are not joyously confident in his forgiveness—I hope the Holy Spirit will use this chapter to roll away that heavy stone. May God's forgiveness flood your heart with the sweet taste of mercy.

Why Is This Stone Here?

Why, when we hear so often about God's forgiveness, and maybe even tell others about it, do we still feel guilty? Our enemy concentrates much of his efforts right here. He is called "the accuser," and he devotes himself—night and day—to accusing us before God (Revelation 12:10).

Zechariah gives us an intimate glimpse of Satan doing this. Zechariah describes Joshua appearing before the angel of the Lord. Joshua wears soiled rags, representing not only his sin but his very best deeds (Isaiah 64:6), and Satan stands "at his right hand to accuse him" (Zechariah 3:1-3). Don't your cheeks burn for Joshua? He is exposed before God. And Satan hovers close to loudly remind everyone of Joshua's guilt and unworthiness. Sound familiar?

Why does Satan accuse us? By oppressing us with guilt, he keeps us from the sweet core of God's heart and drains the joy out of God's good news. Instead of joyfully worshiping God—delighting in his mercy—we shrink away from him in anxiety. We may even quietly resent him. Our suffering reflects to the world a false version of him. If we say we belong to him, and we are anxious and guilty, then he must be an angry, uncompassionate, judgmental God set against sinners. Thus, Satan achieves his greater purpose: he has enticed us to slander God. How many people have turned away from God because those who claim to know him represent him this way?

But in the story Zechariah tells about Joshua, the Lord rebukes Satan. He says, "The Lord rebuke you, O Satan! The Lord who has chosen Jerusalem rebuke you! Is not this a brand plucked from the fire?" (Zechariah 3:2). And the angel gives Joshua new clothes to wear:

> *And the angel said to those who were standing before him, 'Remove the filthy garments from him.' And to him he said, 'Behold, I have taken your iniquity away from you, and I will clothe you with pure vestments.'...So they put a clean turban on his head and clothed him with garments* (Zechariah 3:4-5).

God silences Joshua's enemy, removes Joshua's shame, and clothes Joshua in spotless garments. Can you imagine Joshua's joy? Can you imagine his delight in the mercy of God's heart? God extends to us the same mercy he showed Joshua. Because

God *is* merciful. When he declares himself before Moses, he says, "The Lord, the Lord, a God merciful and gracious, slow to anger, and abounding in steadfast love" (Exodus 34:6). He wants Moses to know that at God's very core is a heart of mercy and steadfast love.

The writer of Lamentations knew this, and he rejoiced that the mercy of God is as dependable as the sunrise: "The steadfast love of the Lord never ceases; his mercies never come to an end; they are new every morning" (Lamentations 3:22-23). A. W. Tozer defines mercy as "the goodness of God confronting human suffering and guilt," and explains, "Forever His mercy stands, a boundless, overwhelming immensity of divine pity and compassion."[17]

Paul says we, like Joshua after his cleansing, will stand before the Lord, "in splendor, without spot or wrinkle or any such thing...holy and without blemish" (Ephesians 5:27). Jesus purchased this for us—splendor before God. This is the JOY of the Christian heart.

When our hearts pound with this kind of joy, we forget ourselves, losing ourselves in glorifying God as trophies of his mercy. Look, we say, look at our God! He is merciful; his kindness knows no end; where have we encountered a beautiful, glorious, merciful heart like this? Love him! Treasure him! When we receive his forgiveness, we become people of irrepressible delight who cannot stop praising and making him known. We overcome our accuser with the word of our testimony and "the blood of the Lamb" (Revelation 12:11).

Let us roll away the guilt of the accuser that steals our joy and kills our testimony. I long for us all to throw down the stone of guilt and take up the joy of the forgiven: those who know the heart of God is not hatred toward sinful men, but mercy; those who take their place at his feast as one more mercy-trophy. May we lift up God's tender heart for the world to see.

But how do we remove this stubborn stone? To tear down

guilt, we need to discern its roots. Our persistent guilt can have a number of sources: unrepented sin, unconfessed sin, false guilt, or pride and unbelief.

Unrepented Sin

To combat guilt, we must first rule out that we are not experiencing legitimate conviction from the Holy Spirit. Sometimes people, while persisting in known sin, lament to me they cannot feel close to God. I try to explain that God may allow the feelings of distance in order to draw their attention to the sin.

Sin is bad for us. We sin when we try to get good things through means God has not blessed: stealing or cheating to get money or possessions; gossiping to make others look bad so we look better; having sex outside marriage to feel loved; controlling people with our anger so they don't hurt us; or getting drunk or high to feel happy. But James tells us God alone gives us good things: "Do not be deceived, my beloved brothers. Every good gift and every perfect gift is from above, coming down from the Father of lights" (James 1:16-17). We are deceived when we think we can get good things by sinful means. Choosing a lifestyle of sin is like playing in a busy street: it's dangerous. The Bible warns about the harmful effects of sin:

- Sin hardens and deceives us (Hebrews 3:13).

- Sin blinds us (1 John 2:11).

- Sin wounds us (Isaiah 1:2-6; 1 Timothy 6:10).

- Sin enslaves us (John 8:34).

- Sin prevents us from knowing God (1 John 3:6).

- Sin separates us from God—for eternity (Mark 9:43).

God's forgiveness does not change these realities. He loves us and desires to forgive us, but he also wants to save us from sin—to pull us off the street. If we belong to him but persist in willful sin, he will attempt to rescue us by causing us great discomfort.

One of the Holy Spirit's jobs is to "convict the world concerning sin" (John 16:8). He presses us to examine our hearts. Is God asking us to do something we refuse to do? Is he pointing out a sin we cherish? Conviction from the Holy Spirit is specific and clear, not vague. He will tell us what he wants us to deal with, and we will have no peace until we comply. David felt this distress when he refused to repent of sin: "When I kept silent, my bones wasted away through my groaning all day long. For day and night your hand was heavy upon me; my strength was dried up as by the heat of summer" (Psalm 32:3-4).

One way we show love for God is by agreeing with him that his ideas about right living constitute the most whole, healthy, and beautiful way to live. We entrust ourselves to him when we say with the psalmist, "You are my Lord; apart from you I have no good thing" (Psalm 16:2 NIV). Loving and trusting him, we stop our sinful attempts to secure happiness by ungodly means. We will not completely stop sinning; sin will still erupt out of us unbidden and unexpected. But sin will not define–characterize—us; we will cease a lifestyle of premeditated sin. And we will no longer feel guilty all the time.

So we remove this kind of guilt-stone by repentance—agreeing with God that our sin hurts him and us, renouncing the sin, and asking God to forgive us and to help us trust him with our needs.

Unconfessed Sin

In Psalm 32 David describes the agony of living with unrepented sin, but he also describes the joy of confession. He finally responds to the Lord's conviction: "I acknowledged my sin to you, and I did not cover my iniquity; I said, 'I will confess my transgressions to the Lord,' and you forgave the iniquity of my sin" (Psalm 32:5). David ends the psalm with exclamations of joy in God's love: "Many are the sorrows of the wicked, but steadfast love surrounds the one who trusts in the Lord. Be glad in the Lord, and rejoice, O righteous, and shout for joy, all you upright in heart!" (Psalm 32:10-11).

Sometimes we keep feeling guilty, even though we have ceased a pattern of sin, because we have not taken time to confess that sin to the Lord, ask for his forgiveness, and receive his mercy deep in our hearts. We live in a time of rushing and distraction. We may throw up prayers asking for forgiveness and hurry on, ignoring our lingering guilt.

We also might put off confession while we try to make up for what we have done wrong. Maybe we think if we do some good things we will appease him before we confess. Doing this, we can put off indefinitely the opportunity to confess our sin and receive forgiveness.

We can only tear down this kind of guilt-stone by SLOWING DOWN. Unhurried and still, we confess our sin to him. Continuing in quiet, we allow time for lingering guilt or fear of condemnation to surface. If it does, we talk to the Lord about it. It can help to imagine putting on the pure garments Jesus bought for us. I like to make the sign of the cross over myself, as a symbol of Jesus's crucifixion paying for my sin. I also like to pray this verse, "If we confess our sins, he is faithful and just to forgive us our sins and to cleanse us from all unrighteousness" (1 John 1:9) to help my heart trust that God wants to forgive me.

Whatever it takes, we must try not to leave our time of confession with a vague hope that God will forgive us and a creeping feeling of guilt gnawing at our insides. We want to rise from prayer with joy in God's forgiving heart. If we cannot come to this place on our own, we must seek others to pray with us (James 5:16).

False Guilt

If after confessing and repenting of sin, we still feel a cloud of guilt we cannot put a name to, we may suffer from false guilt. We can name real sin. False guilt differs because we cannot name the sin producing it. We don't know what to confess; we just feel horribly guilty. False guilt is guilt we should not carry.

Children are prone to blame themselves for things out of their control: the divorce of their parents, the death of a sibling, or sexual abuse, for example. On top of that, the enemy may take advantage of this childhood tendency to tell us accusatory lies, intensifying our false guilt.

I have a friend whose older brother died in a family car accident. My friend, although she was a small child at the time of accident, felt guilty for her brother's death. The enemy may have said to my friend, "You caused this. You are responsible for your brother's death. Look what you have done." She suffered from dark moods and self-condemnation for many years, and her story is not uncommon. Children who suffer abuse are particularly prone to believe the abuse was their fault.

Sometimes our parents or others may even—intentionally or unintentionally—blame us for things that are not our fault. This happened to me. While I was in the hospital after my head-injury, my parents left my eight-month-old sister Heather with our great-grandmother. As I was growing up I often heard my mom talk about how terrible she felt for leaving my sister like that.

I was in my forties before I realized the painful false guilt I carried about this. The enemy rooted this lie so deeply in me it grew tentacles; I did not only feel guilty for taking my parents away from my sister for a week, I subconsciously believed my existence deprived my sister of what she needed from my parents, as if by breathing in her vicinity I stole her oxygen. I finally realized this lie produced some of the oppressive sense of shame I felt before God. I wept buckets before the Lord as he washed away this stone of false guilt and gave me a more reasonable sense of what happened at the time of my accident. If you suffer from false guilt, you will need the Lord's help— like I did—and possibly the help of others to discern the lies you have believed. You may need to grieve, renounce lies, and receive truth from the Lord. The Lord may heal your false guilt in a one-time event such as prayer for healing of memories, which I explain in another chapter, or you may enter a process of choosing to cling to the Lord's truth many times a day until the feelings of false guilt go away.

Pride and Unbelief

Stones of guilt can come from pride and unbelief. A.W. Tozer refers to this type of guilt: "Could our failure to capture the pure joy of mercy consciously experienced be the result of our unbelief or our ignorance, or both?"[18]

We know we suffer this kind of guilt when we work ourselves to exhaustion, trying never to sin, trying to be good enough for God. We are especially susceptible to this kind of guilt if our families expected perfection from us. If we had a family like this, we tried to be good to avoid rejection, anger, or condemnation. But when we transfer that dynamic into our relationship with God—as we naturally do—we keep guilt between his heart and ours.

Trying to be good to earn his love, we fail to trust the righteousness God gives us through Jesus. We try to make our own. In this way, we allow our fear of condemnation to back us into pride.

And working so hard to be perfect, we live out of unbelief. We hear God's love differs from the love of our parents or other authority figures, but we don't believe it. Instead, we strive to be perfect, to have no need for forgiveness.

So we remove this kind of guilt-stone by repenting of pride and unbelief. I know this seems counter-intuitive; if we feel overwhelmed with guilt, we confess pride? Yes. Believing God will not forgive us is a twisted form of pride; rejecting the sufficiency of his cross, we want our own righteousness to bring him. If we realize this about ourselves, we must humble ourselves, confess to him our foolish pride, and renounce trusting our own righteousness. Only then can we celebrate the forgiveness he offers us.

I saw this once—so beautifully—in a time of healing prayer. We were praying for a lovely young woman who hated herself intensely. Though it was difficult to urge her to do it because we had deep compassion for her shame, we believed the Holy Spirit was inviting her to confess her sin so she could know God's forgiveness. She began to confess the sins of a lifetime spent in addiction and self-destruction, and the words came out of her in a torrent. I have tears in my eyes today remembering part of what poured out of her heart—her plea for the Lord to forgive her for not *believing* he could forgive her. She left us saying she felt lighter than air.

After repenting of our pride and unbelief, we exercise faith by seeing ourselves in Christ's righteousness (Galatians 3:27) and resting in God's presence with no fear of condemnation (Romans 8:1). Paul says he counts all that was to his credit as "rubbish, in order that I may gain Christ and be found in him, not having a righteousness of my own that comes from the law, but that which comes through faith in Christ, the righteousness from God that depends on faith" (Philippians 3:8-9).

The following exercises will help you discern the source of any guilt-stones standing between your heart and God's heart and tear them down. May you come alive to the joy of *experiencing* God's forgiveness.

Spiritual Exercises for Chapter Five

Unrepented Sin

1. Prayerfully read Psalm 139:23-24: "Search me, O God, and know my heart! Try me and know my thoughts! And see if there be any grievous way in me, and lead me in the way everlasting!"

2. Sit before God in silence, waiting for him to surface any areas of sin he may urge you to confess. When something comes to mind, confess it aloud to him, praying something like this:

> Father, I have sinned against you by _____ _____. I confess this sin to you now and ask you to forgive me. I praise you that "with you there is forgiveness" (Psalm 130:4), and I trust you sent Jesus to die in my place so you can forgive me. I praise you for your mercy and forgiveness. I renounce this sin now. Please help me not to sin this way any longer. I put on the righteousness of Jesus and I rejoice that I stand before you "in splendor, without spot or wrinkle or any such thing" (Ephesians 5:27).

Try not to end your time of confession until you are able to be confident in the Lord's forgiveness. If this is not possible, seek someone to pray with you about this.

3. If the Lord brings to mind an area of sin you are not ready to turn away from, ask him to help you. Invite him into your thinking. You might pray, "Lord, I know you say this is a sin, but I am not ready to let it go. I think I need _____ to be okay. Please fill me with your Holy Spirit and help me to see things as you see them. Show

me how I have been deceived. I invite you to change my heart. Please help me!" Please also seek prayer and help from others. You may make this verse from Psalm 119 your prayer, "I will run in the way of your commandments when you enlarge my heart!" (v. 32).

Unconfessed Sin

If you have left certain sin patterns behind, but have never confessed those sins and rejoiced in the Lord's forgiveness, please allow this exercise to help you do this.

1. Prayerfully read Psalm 25. Reread verse 7 where David talks about the "sins of his youth." Sit with the Lord and ask him to show you the sins you have left behind with his help. Make a list in your journal.

2. One at a time, confess these sins to the Lord and ask for his forgiveness. You may make David's prayer yours, "For your name's sake, O Lord, pardon my guilt, for it is great" (v. 11).

3. Remember God's promises: "If we confess our sins, he is faithful and just to forgive us our sins and to cleanse us from all unrighteousness" (1 John 1:9); and "as far as the east is from the west, so far does he remove our transgressions from us" (Psalm 103:12-13). Ask him to show you how he sees you.

4. Thank and praise God for forgiving you.

False Guilt

1. Read Romans 8:1; Isaiah 1:18; and Zephaniah 3:17. Ask the Lord to show you if you can delight in these promises, or if you still suffer under guilt or shame. Ask him to help

you see if you carry false guilt. Sit quietly with him and wait for him to surface anything.

2. If God reveals something to you, sit with him and allow your emotions to surface.

3. Forgive, if you are able, anyone who put false guilt on you.

4. Ask the Lord to forgive you for carrying this guilt and for not accepting his gift of righteousness.

5. Give to the Lord any lies you believed and ask him to speak his truth to you.

Pride and Unbelief

1. Prayerfully read Philippians 3:7-9. Then read Isaiah 64:6: "We have all become like one who is unclean, and all our righteous deeds are like a polluted garment."

2. Ask the Lord to help you see if you have assumed God could not forgive you and have tried to make yourself good enough for him. What have you trusted to make yourself acceptable? What have you chosen to "put on" in place of the righteousness that he offers? Write down anything he shows you. Confess to the Lord these false ways of overcoming guilt or shame.

3. Read Zechariah 3:1-5. Put yourself in Joshua's place and ask the Lord to clothe you with the purity Jesus purchased for you so he might present you to God, "without spot or wrinkle or any such thing...holy and without blemish," (Ephesians 5:26-27).

4. Spend time thanking the Lord for forgiving you and for the spotlessness he gives you.

Discussion Questions for Chapter Five:
The Stone of Guilt

(You do not need to name any sins during the following discussion; we are talking about the difficulties we may have with guilt, not specific areas of sin.)

1. Have you ever had a difficult time believing God forgives you? Why do you think this is?

2. Do you remember a time when you were forgiven, by God or by someone else? What emotions did you experience?

3. Have you "tasted" the Lord's mercy?

4. Have you experienced the conviction of the Holy Spirit? How would you describe his "voice" when he confronts you about sin?

5. How do you typically approach confession? Do you think that you take enough time to receive forgiveness from God?

6. Do you have any experience with false guilt?

7. Were you able, after working through the spiritual exercises at the end of this chapter, to be relieved of guilt?

Chapter Six
The Stone of Unforgiveness

"He has sent me to bind up the brokenhearted."
~ Isaiah 61:1

*"Forgive us our debts,
as we also have forgiven our debtors."*
~ Matthew 6:12

Some nights you might hear loud music at my house. If you peeked through the kitchen window you would see my husband and me be-bopping around the kitchen with our three children. When they were small, we often chose an album by Martina McBride, and I remember one bittersweet line pierced me every time. McBride's crystalline voice sings a list of joyous things: confetti, snow, laughter, and—perfect unbroken hearts.[19] I held their little hands and looked down at their trusting, joy-filled faces, and my heart ached. I longed for them to keep their perfect hearts, so free to give and receive love. But I knew almost no one does. Before we get far, someone breaks our heart.

This was true for me. My heart broke when kids teased me at school, when boys in my class threw my custom-made helmet into the woods where it was lost, and when my uncle killed my aunt and cousin. My heart still gets chipped and cracked every so often.

I feel sorrow because your heart has likely been broken too. Your story may hold more pain than mine. But my sorrow cannot compare to how the Lord feels. Isaiah tells us when the

Lord's people hurt, he shares our pain: "In all their affliction he was afflicted" (Isaiah 63:9) and, "Surely he has borne our griefs and carried our sorrows" (Isaiah 53:4). I pray as we talk about forgiveness you can trust I am sensitive to the pain you may be in and God suffers with you.

But I bring joyful news: With God a broken heart doesn't have to stay broken. Just as we saw death working backward, we will see how God restores a wounded heart to the joy of the hearts pounding in the dancing bodies of my children.

Stones of Unforgiveness

When someone wounds us, we often respond by constructing a protective wall around our hurting heart with stones of unforgiveness. If you have done this, you may feel I am about to ask you to tear down the very thing keeping you safe, that removing stones of unforgiveness will leave you vulnerable to more hurt. I hope to explain that though unforgiveness feels like a defense, it does not actually protect us; instead it *binds* us to those who hurt us and *blocks* us from receiving the healing love of our Father.

The power to move a heart from broken to bountiful, from hurting to healed, comes through forgiveness. If, after reading this chapter, you seek to forgive those who have hurt you, you will be choosing the only path from *victim*—a person hidden behind a stone wall of self-protection—to *victor*—a joyful person free to love and be loved in relation to God and others. May God give you courage to proceed.

False Concepts of Forgiveness

False ideas about forgiveness can make it seem distasteful, so I want to clear them away.

When someone says to you, "I'm sorry," don't you feel

compelled to say, "It's okay"? Culturally, we consider this the appropriate response to an apology. But when we say, "It's okay," we mean, "No worries. What you did wasn't so bad." Our, "It's okay," minimizes and dismisses the offense. This response befits excusing a friend for arriving ten minutes late for lunch.

But what happens if our spouse has an affair? Or our business partner cheats us out of our retirement? Or our dad used to beat us? If we mistakenly think God requires us to say, "It's okay," in these situations, forgiveness will be a bitter pill. But this is a misconception.

When we forgive we do not excuse or condone someone's evil actions. An offense requiring forgiveness is—de facto—a sinful offense. Through the process of forgiveness, we say the offense was NOT okay. We say our offender's actions were wrong, even evil, and require not dismissal, but *forgiveness.* Forgiveness involves deep honesty about our pain and specificity about the sin of our offender.

We also misunderstand forgiveness when we assume it always means the restoration of the status quo in the relationship. In fact, extending forgiveness may free us to end or insist on change in a destructive relationship. Please be encouraged. I will not ask you to minimize someone's sin or to stay in an abusive relationship.

True Forgiveness

When someone sins against us, our pain grows into anger and desire for retribution. True forgiveness is the process of *releasing* and *renouncing* our anger, bitterness, or rage. Seen this way, forgiveness does not happen because we inexplicably work up warm feelings for our offender. Forgiveness happens when we choose to lay down our right to be angry.

But where? And how?

We must come, through our heart's imagination, to the

cross. Jesus's cross is God's reckoning place for sin—our sin *and* the sin done against us. At his cross we are helped toward forgiveness because here we find Jesus paying the penalty for the sin of our offender *and* sharing our suffering.

God's fury over sin fell upon Jesus: "He was pierced for our transgressions; he was crushed for our iniquities" (Isaiah 53:5). Standing before the cross, our hearts absorb God's estimation of the evil done to us. He does not dismiss the sin of our adulterous spouse, our abusive dad, or our treacherous business partner—God does not say, "It's okay." Because of Jesus's suffering we understand, in God's judgment, people who commit such acts deserve tortured death and hell. We can allow God's anger on our behalf to comfort us.

But at the cross we also see—flowing from God's loving and forgiving heart—*Jesus* receiving the punishment for the sin of the one who hurt us. The cross of Jesus potentially frees him or her from suffering the consequences of sin in hell.

No pain another's sin has caused us surpasses the agony Jesus and his Father endured at the cross for that same sin. So at the cross we find Jesus sharing our pain; we can remember he "has borne our griefs and carried our sorrows" (Isaiah 53:4) and allow our pain to flow into him.

When my children get hurt, I wrap them in my arms and hold them close. I want them to know that they are not alone in their pain, and that if possible I would take their hurt into myself to spare them. This instinct comes from God's father-heart. Only he—wondrously—*can* absorb our pain into the suffering of his Son. In prayer at the cross we allow Jesus to absorb our wounds, in the embrace of the Father, so by "his wounds we are healed" (Isaiah 53:5).

At the cross, forgiveness becomes an act of worship. As we accept the wrath he poured out on Jesus as sufficient punishment for the sins of those who have hurt us, we must love him. We love him for being just—full of fury over injustice and sin—and yet so loving he unleashes that fury upon himself to forgive sinners. And we love him for descending from glory to the filth of earth to absorb our suffering—to carry our sorrows—so that we are not ever alone, no matter what we have suffered. To forgive our enemies is to celebrate God.

So at the cross, the stone of unforgiveness comes down as we release our pain *and* the sin of our offender into Jesus. When I pray with people to help them forgive, I ask them to picture Jesus on the cross and release their anger into the anger of God. Then I ask them to see Jesus sharing their pain. The spiritual exercises for this chapter will guide you in doing these things.

When we have forgiven someone, we can acknowledge their sin hurt us and we were once angry at them, but we no longer feel anger or desire vengeance. We can experience contentment—even happiness—if our offender chooses repentance and God forgives them. We can celebrate God's forgiving heart by desiring for our enemies to escape the eternal consequences of their sin on the Day of Judgment. Eventually, forgiveness makes way for the Holy Spirit to heal our hearts so completely that we may, with his help, pray to "love our enemies and do good to those who hate us" (Luke 6:27).

The Danger of Unforgiveness

God commands us to forgive: "And whenever you stand praying, forgive, if you have anything against anyone, so that your Father also who is in heaven may forgive you your trespasses" (Mark 11:25). But why? Can't he heal our hearts a different way?

God wants us to forgive because unforgiveness is bad for us: it makes us sick—emotionally and sometimes physically—puts relationships we value at risk, gives the demonic power to oppress us, and binds us to those who have hurt us.

Imagine your soul as a lovely home filled with your treasures.

Fine works of art represent people you love; a glass-blowing studio, wood shop, or gourmet kitchen represents your gifts and talents. Now imagine you invite something wild and destructive into your home, a bear or a rhinoceros. Though you intend to give that ferocious thing access to the porch to guard your valuables, you find you cannot contain the beast. It tears through your home, crushing and destroying your treasures without regard for restraints. Unforgiveness works like this in our souls. Once we let it in, nothing is safe.

When we do not forgive, we nurture hatred, rage, and bitterness in our souls. We intend to focus that anger on the person we do not want to forgive. But anger moves through us like a wild animal; it doesn't respect restraints. We grow angry at people we love, angry at God, and angry at ourselves, and we damage these relationships. Our anger clenches our heart like a fist so God's love cannot get in and our love cannot get out; we choke our gifts and fail to share them.

Unresolved anger also gives Satan's demons permission to attach themselves to us. Paul warned the Ephesians, "'In your anger do not sin': Do not let the sun go down while you are still angry, and do not give the devil a foothold" (Ephesians 4:26-27 NIV). Nurturing anger is like setting out bait for the demonic. Eventually, they will come to feed, and demonically empowered anger will spread through our soul. In this sense, forgiveness is a spiritual weapon the Lord gives us to protect us from oppression by the evil one.

The effects of unforgiveness are not limited to emotional and spiritual problems; unforgiveness can also make us physically sick. Leanne Payne tells a story that is a good example of this. A friend of hers suffered from painful, crippling arthritis. This woman made her invalid neighbor lunch every day. But each and every day, just before Leanne's friend went out the door with the food, the neighbor would call on the telephone to ask if she were coming. Leanne's friend got angrier and angrier about these phone calls, and her arthritis worsened. But one day as a group gathered to pray for the healing of Leanne's friend's arthritis, the invalid neighbor came powerfully to her friend's mind. Leanne's friend forgave the invalid woman for her demanding neediness, and the arthritis disappeared.[20]

Unforgiveness Binds Us to Our Enemies

Though we believe unforgiveness protects us, it actually binds us to those who have hurt us. Susan's story may help me explain. Susan's father chose alcohol over his children, and Susan entered adulthood wounded and resentful. At sixty, though she has become a Christian, she lives in pain, always watching for a new offense from her father to fuel her anger. She thinks about him a lot, scrutinizing what he does with his time and money. She waits for him to experience remorse, stop drinking, and give her the love she longs for. Sometimes she fantasizes about him experiencing an accident or hospitalization that will wake him up to the ways he has hurt and neglected her.

Susan's anger closes her heart, like a fist wrapped around an IOU, and God's father-love can't get in to heal her. Her friends and family find her moody, irritable, and sulky.

Only forgiveness can free Susan of the effects of this wounding relationship. When Susan forgives her earthly father, her closed heart will open to soak in the love of her heavenly Father. Then when her dad comes to mind, Susan may feel affection toward him and sorrow for him that he has wasted his life on alcohol, but forgiveness will have drained away her anger and pain. She may go days without thinking about him, and other people will find Susan more relaxed, able to laugh more freely, and less easily offended. She will no longer be bound to him; forgiveness will have freed her.

Forgiveness and the Kingdom of God

Above God's concern for our welfare, God's command for us to forgive flows from his character and the nature of his kingdom. God forgives. Jesus—God himself—hangs in shameful pain on the cross, suffering the hatred and jeering of his murderers, and says, "Father, forgive them, for they know not what they do" (Luke 23:34).

Our forgiving King, in love and generosity, wants men and women to share his kingdom: "Fear not, little flock, for it is your Father's good pleasure to give you the kingdom" (Luke 12:32). But in our sin we cannot enter it. God must wash every person who will spend eternity with him in the forgiveness he purchased through the death of his Son.

If we enter God's kingdom through forgiveness, purchased by the tortured death of Jesus, we must radiate forgiveness. Imagine a land where everyone wears white. What if we came wearing black? Or picture a kingdom where the people greet one another with kisses. What if we greeted others with a slap? We embody incongruity like this if we want to live in the kingdom of God, yet refuse to forgive.

Jesus paints a picture of this problem in the parable of the unforgiving servant (Matthew 18:21-35). The master forgives the servant a fortune of debt. But the servant throws a man who owes *him* pocket-change into jail. The forgiven man fails to recognize the fragrance in the air he breathes or to honor his master by adopting his generous and forgiving spirit. Jesus shows us what we look like when we want God to forgive us, but we do not want to forgive one another. At the end of the parable the master restores the servant's debt and puts him in prison. Jesus warns, "So also my heavenly Father will do to every one of you, if you do not forgive your brother from your heart" (Matthew 18:35).

Elsewhere Jesus reiterates this warning: "For if you forgive others their trespasses, your heavenly Father will also forgive you, but if you do not forgive others their trespasses, neither will your Father forgive your trespasses" (Matthew 6:14-15).

God commands us to forgive because he forgives, and in his kingdom we must reflect the character of the forgiving King, just as Jesus did on the cross. If we choose unforgiveness to protect ourselves, we don't fit in this kingdom.

But there is more!

The Hope of the Kingdom of God

Part of the joy of being a child of God is our hopeful anticipation of the day we will live in the fullness of his kingdom. This hope gives us power to forgive, the same power that helped Jesus, who "For the joy that was set before him endured the cross" (Hebrews 12:2).

If we belong to God, dear friends, we live with the hope of heaven (Luke 12:32); we are the richest people alive. No one can steal anything from us that God will not restore in his kingdom. Someone may take our dignity, our innocence, our loved one, our riches, even our life, but we cannot suffer a permanent loss.

When we enter God's kingdom at the end of time, he will wipe every tear from our eyes (Isaiah 25:8) and fill us with joy (Psalm 16:11). We will live in a happiness unimaginable to us now. Paul voices this hope: "For this light momentary affliction is preparing for us an eternal weight of glory beyond all comparison, as we look not to the things that are seen but to the things that are unseen. For the things that are seen are transient, but the things that are unseen are eternal" (2 Corinthians 4:17-18). In other words, anything anyone takes from us, we were going to lose anyway because everything on earth is passing away. But no matter how "poor" someone's sin makes us, we remain rich beyond measure.

And the news gets better yet. We do not have to wait for

heaven to enjoy all of the benefits of being God's children, because God has promised to redeem everything that happens to us, no matter how evil, and use it for our good and the good of others: "And we know that for those who love God all things work together for good" (Romans 8:28). Think of the story of Joseph, whose brothers sell him as a slave to Egypt. When Joseph forgives his brothers, he says to them, "As for you, you meant evil against me, but God meant it for good, to bring it about that many people should be kept alive, as they are today" (Genesis 50:20). Joseph's forgiveness flows out of his understanding of God's power to use even evil actions for good in his kingdom.

The coming kingdom of God means chapters of pain and loss do not define our story: no matter how bad it gets, God is not finished writing our story toward the best, most joyful ending. And on our way there God can soak up every drop of our suffering to use for our good and for the blessing of others. I pray this hope empowers our forgiveness.

The Power Comes from God

I have one last word of encouragement. We are not capable of forgiving the people who have deeply wounded us. We speak the truth when we cry out, "I cannot forgive." But Jesus is willing, through his Holy Spirit inside us, to empower us to forgive—to forgive through us. He would not command us to forgive if this were not true.

Many people who pray for others for healing affirm this truth. Leanne Payne says when someone tells her they cannot forgive, she acknowledges the truth of what they are saying and then goes on to tell the wounded person the power to forgive will not come from them, but from Jesus. She tells them they will receive the power they need from the Holy Spirit, as Jesus promised in Acts 1:8; a power so strong they will be able to forgive even the worst imaginable offenses.[21]

My grandmother experienced this when my uncle John murdered her daughter and granddaughter. Friends of the family gathered across the street from the bloody crime scene on the day of the murders. John was on the loose. My grandmother's friends said, "We need to pray for John," and gathered in a circle holding hands, stretching out their hands for my grandmother to join them. My grandmother couldn't do it. She cried out to God, "O God, this is too much for me—You take care of John."[22]

Months later she realized she did not have any unforgiveness toward John. "How can this be, God?" she asked. He reminded her of the time she had prayed for him to take care of John, and he spoke to her heart, "Right then I took all the responsibility off you and carried it myself."[23] God gave my grandmother the power to forgive the unforgiveable; in fact, he forgave for her and through her. He is willing to do the same for all of us.

If someone has broken your heart, and if you have built a wall with stones of unforgiveness to "protect" yourself, I pray this chapter has inspired you to seek the Lord's help to tear them down. I pray the joy of God's kingdom and his indwelling Holy Spirit empowers you. I hope you find comfort seeing there is a place for your pain, where Jesus shares your suffering, and a place for your anger, where God's fury has landed on Jesus—at the cross. I hope you will trust unforgiveness does not protect you but instead keeps you in the role of victim, bound to your offender, and I hope through God's help you will become a victor—free to receive the healing love of God and give it to others.

Spiritual Exercises for Chapter Six

Seeking God's Forgiveness

1. Prayerfully read and meditate upon the parable of the unforgiving servant found in Matthew 18:21-35. Put yourself in the place of the servant and celebrate for a moment the sins the Lord has forgiven you.

2. Ask him if he would like you to confess or repent of any sin. Sit quietly with him and wait for him to bring anything to mind.

3. Confess any sins he has revealed. Renounce these sins (meaning, determine in your heart to turn away from them with the Lord's help and ask for his power to help you not repeat these sins).

4. Read 1 John 1:9, and thank God for his forgiveness. Bless him for being a forgiving King.

Forgiving "Lesser" offenses

1. Read Mark 11:25 and Matthew 6:9, 12, 14-15. Ask the Lord to search your heart and reveal to you anyone whom you have not forgiven. Make a list of these people.

2. Ask the Lord to pour his Holy Spirit into you to enable you to forgive.

3. If the offenses seem "small" and you feel empowered to forgive, speak your forgiveness aloud to the Lord, praying something like this:

> Lord, I come to you now and I bring you the sin of _____ against me. _____ has sinned against me

by _____ (*name their sin*). I release this sin into your body on the cross, and I am content to have your suffering pay the penalty for this sin. I also confess to you the anger or bitterness I have held in my heart toward _____; I release my anger and unforgiveness into your body on the cross as well. I repent of that anger, and I ask you to forgive me for nurturing it in my heart. I stand before your cross and I forgive _____. I pray for you to help me, Lord, to be angry with him/her no longer and to love him/her with your love. I pray for you to bless _____ with every spiritual blessing in Christ. Amen.

4. Do this for each person on your list whose sins fit into this category of lesser sins.

The Cross Exercise for Greater Offenses

1. If someone has sinned against you greatly, I recommend working through the following exercise to prepare your heart for forgiveness. At the end of this chapter, please find the picture of a cross. On the left-hand side of the picture notice the heading "_____'s Sins Against Me," (go ahead and fill in the name in the blank) and on the right-hand, "What These Sins Cost Me." Please make a copy of this diagram on a separate sheet of paper so you can throw it away when you are finished, and so you will have the copy provided here if you want to come back to it in the future.

2. Ask the Lord to help you list this person's sins against you. Be honest and direct. You are not sinning against them by

being clear about the ways they have hurt you. As you make this list, ask the Lord to help you see what this person's sins have cost you. You may need to take some time to grieve as you write these things out. I know it is hard, but it is important for you to be in touch with your true heart at this point. Remember, "The Lord is near to the brokenhearted and saves the crushed in spirit" (Psalm 34:18).

3. As you proceed, ask the Lord to show you ways he has been moving in your life to redeem and heal the wounds you sustained. Can you see he brought something good out of a tragedy or did he send someone to love you in ways the person who hurt you could not? If he shows you anything, write this on the back of your page. It is okay if you cannot write anything at this time.

4. When you have completed the diagram, work through each offense, one at a time, forgiving the person. You may use the prayer below. You can do this on your own if you feel comfortable. However, I recommend having someone present to pray with you.

A Prayer to Extend Forgiveness

Heavenly Father, I humble myself before you. I have courage to come into your presence because "you are a God ready to forgive, gracious and merciful, slow to anger and abounding in steadfast love" (Nehemiah 9:17). I love you for joyfully forgiving me. I know the forgiveness you offer me came at great cost because you allowed the blood of your beloved Son to be poured out for the forgiveness my sins and the sins of others (Matthew 26:28). I thank you for loving me this much.

I confess to you, Father, the unforgiveness I have held

in my heart toward _____, who has
hurt me deeply. I am angry at _____ for the sins of
_____ he/she has
committed against me. These sins have cost me greatly.
They have cost me _____

_____.

I am grieved over these losses, and I pour out my
broken-heartedness before you now because you are the
Father of mercies and the God of all comfort and you
will wipe every tear from my eyes (2 Corinthians 1:3;
Isaiah 25:8).

*(Take as much time as you need here to tell the Lord
your sorrows and to grieve before him.)*

I confess before you, Father, I do not have the power
to forgive this person. Please pour out your Holy Spirit
upon me (Acts 1:8) and give me your forgiving love so I
can forgive_____ *(name the person).*

Jesus, I stand before your cross. I see you in your
suffering, and I thank you for sharing my pain with me;
your word says, "Surely he has born our griefs and carried
our sorrows" (Isaiah 53:4). I love you, Jesus, for making
me one with you and for meeting me in my pain. Thank you
that I am not alone in my suffering. Thank you that here at
your cross I can release my anger, bitterness, hatred, and
unforgiveness toward _____.
I ask you to let all of these feelings flow out of me and
into your body.

*(Take time now to allow your anger and unforgiveness
to flow into Jesus on the cross.)*

Jesus, in light of your cross, I renounce my anger and
bitterness toward _____. I pray for you to

forgive me for holding on to these feelings. I acknowledge that your suffering covers _____'s sins as well as my own, and I am content to have it be so. I forgive _____ for _____, and I ask you, Father, to forgive him/her so he/she will not suffer the eternal consequences of those sins when he/she faces you on the Day of Judgment. Thank you, Father, for giving me your Holy Spirit and enabling me to forgive. Thank you for the freedom and healing my heart will experience as a result of this forgiveness. I pray you will work in me so I will be able to pray blessing upon _____, as you have said we must bless those who curse us and pray for those who persecute us.

And now, loving Father, I trust you with the wounds and losses I have suffered because of this person's sins. I trust you to heal my body, restore my soul, strengthen my spirit, and renew my mind. I know there is nothing that can separate me from your love and no matter what I have suffered, it cannot compare to the eternal glory, joy, and pleasures I will experience at your right hand in your kingdom (Romans 8:38-39; 2 Corinthians 4:17; Psalm 16:11). I choose to fix my eyes not on what is seen, but on what is unseen, and I rejoice in your redemption of all things to work for my good (Romans 8:28). Amen.

Discussion Questions for Chapter Six:
The Stone of Unforgiveness

1. Why do you think unforgiveness feels like self-protection?

2. What was your understanding of forgiveness before reading this chapter? How do you think about it now?

3. Do you know someone who has been eaten up by unforgiveness? Describe your experience with this person. (Please don't use names.)

4. Do you know someone who has been able to forgive what seems unforgiveable? Describe your experience with this person. (Again, no names please).

5. Jasona equates forgiveness with freedom. Describe your thoughts or responses to this idea.

6. Describe your experience with extending forgiveness. What have you found easy? What have you found difficult?

7. Discuss your experiences with the spiritual exercises for this chapter.

PREPARING TO FORGIVE

| _____'s (Name) Sins against Me | What These Sins Cost Me |

Chapter Seven
The Stone of Self–Hatred

"You knitted me together in my mother's womb.
I praise you, for I am fearfully
and wonderfully made."
~ Psalm 139:13-14

"My father and my mother have forsaken me,
but the Lord will take me in."
~ Psalm 27:10

"You shall love your neighbor as yourself."
~ Matthew 22:39

"Whoever does not accept himself
is engrossed with himself."
~ Leanne Payne[24]

My son Jonathan went through a phase at age six when he would say every few days, "I like being me!" or "I am happy being myself. Are you happy being you?" One day he had to answer the question, "What is something special about you?" for a school assignment. He thought for a minute then said happily, "That I'm alive!"

When I hear him say these things, I feel a burst of joy. I delight that my son finds it good to be alive, and my joy reflects the heart of our heavenly Father toward us. We bring him joy when we delight in being alive as his children.

What about you? If Jonathan asked, "Are you happy being you?" what would you say? I hope, and our Father desires, you would answer, "Yes!"

I know, however, many of us would answer that question with uncertainty or negativity. I have counselled many Christians, and I find most of us live with some measure of shame, leading to either self-rejection or full-blown self-hatred.

Charles Kraft agrees: "As I talk to people about their self-image, I find that the vast majority of them at least dislike, if not hate, this person they are supposed to love."[25]

In this chapter we will address this formidable stone: the stone of self-hatred. I earnestly hope the Lord will tear down this painful stone for you—if it sits in the wall between his heart and yours—so your heart will heal through gracious and humble self-acceptance. Until this happens self-hatred suffocates the person God had in mind when he imagined you to life, and the world suffers the want of the inestimable gifts God wants to give us through you—yes, you.

Why Do We Hate Ourselves?

We don't enter life with the maturity to accept ourselves. But when we cry and someone meets our needs with tenderness, we learn our needs are valid. As our caretakers hold and touch us, we learn we belong. So as our mothers and fathers respond to us with compassion and attentiveness, a sense of our worth develops within us.

Through toddlerhood, childhood, and adolescence, we require constant love and affirmation to grow into self-acceptance. In this way, growing children resemble a vase formed on a potter's wheel. The wet lump of clay grows as the firm and gentle hands of the potter hold it through the whole process of its formation. And children require kind, steady, and attentive nurture through every stage of their development to enter adulthood with a secure sense of self.

But even when our parents have provided all this, the assaults of the world and our enemy, like rocks flung at the soft clay in the hands of the potter, can damage our fledgling sense of self, and the stone of self-hatred or self-rejection can set in regardless.

And in some families—through inability, neglect, or abuse—we are deprived of what we need to build a healthy self-acceptance. In these homes, mothers and fathers whom God designed to affirm and bless us into maturity instead crush our fragile sense of self, confirming—either directly through abuse or indirectly through neglect—our terrible suspicions about our unworthiness. When the battering of the world and the attacks of our enemy ratify this condemning verdict, we cement self-hatred into the wall around our heart.

On top of all this, some of us have been taught the Bible affirms this negative view of ourselves. So where the Church could have been a voice of affirmation in the sea of destructive messages we received, instead it confirmed our shame. Kraft refers to such teachings as "Worm Theologies,"[26] theologies emphasizing so heavily our unworthiness and depravity that the reality that God died to save us—attesting to our tremendous value in spite of our sin—does not reach our hearts. Instead we embrace a false humility, a perpetually critical and harsh self-view, and call that Christian maturity.

I call this form of self-hatred false humility because—counter-intuitively—self-absorption and twisted pride lie behind it. I will explain in a minute, and I hope to help you see true humility, while never denying or sugar-coating our sin, enables us to accept ourselves in light of God's loving acceptance of us, freeing us to be joyful worshipers and to take our place in service to him in his kingdom.

So, because our parents were not able or willing to help us grow in self-acceptance, because we suffered rejections and wounds from life in this fallen world, or because we were taught that self-rejection was biblical, we may find stones of self-hatred or self-rejection blocking our hearts from soaking in God's love.

The Truth About Self–Acceptance

The early church fathers taught self-acceptance as a virtue. I do not know why today's church has abandoned this practice, but I yearn for us to recover this emphasis because the fruit of humble self-acceptance blesses the whole world. I hope you will come to agree with me.

Listen for the echoes of self-acceptance in Paul, who could say he was the worst of sinners (1 Timothy 1:15) and also affirm, "I live by faith in the Son of God who *loved me and gave himself for me*" (Galatians 2:20, emphasis added).

Paul based his life on his confidence that Jesus went to the cross because he loved Paul—a simple yet elusive truth. True self-acceptance never denies we are sinners, but it does free us to joyfully receive into the deepest places of our heart the truth Paul celebrates in Romans: "God shows his love for us in that while we were still sinners, Christ died for us" (Romans 5:8).

Paul knew that even as he rebelled against God and persecuted Christians, God loved him and gave his beloved Son over to painful death to rescue him. Paul trusted God had made a way for Paul to enter his kingdom, not out of obligation, but out of love: "For God *so loved* the world, that he gave his only Son, that whoever believes in him should not perish but have eternal life" (John 3:16, emphasis added).

And what was the result of Paul's self-acceptance? He wrote much of the New Testament and spread the gospel to the Gentiles. The church you attend today exists to some degree because of the ministry of Paul. What if Paul, having been saved by Jesus, had slunk away in shame, "knowing" he could never amount to anything in the kingdom of God because of his past? What if Paul had wasted his life in self-hatred, never able to forgive himself for what he had done to Christ's church? *Can you imagine what would have been lost?* Can you see the crippling power of stones of self-hatred and self-rejection and the immeasurable loss to us all when these stones crush just one of us?

When we have not accepted ourselves, where God intends there to be an *essential* human person like Paul—someone using God-given gifts for God's life-giving purposes—there is instead a void, a black hole of self-hatred, diminishing everyone near it.

I see this in families where one person suffers with a serious addiction—an extreme expression of self-hatred. In the family, where the person should be giving and receiving love and other good gifts, the family instead experiences a vacuum: money disappears, children are neglected, parents' hearts are broken, jobs are lost, cars are wrecked, and hopes are destroyed. All of this loss results from the addict trying to drown the pain of self-hatred through the temporary pleasure of addiction while refusing to take his God-given place in the family, the community, and the world. The painful void where God intended his or her life to be shouts of the value of each and every person.

When we do not accept ourselves, we abdicate our place in God's world. We refuse to be. And the world aches for whatever God planned to offer through us—our love, laughter, wisdom, strength, beauty, and kindness—our unique reflection of his image.

For this reason I feel passionate about confronting all that keeps us rejecting ourselves; these things keep us *self*-focused and keep stones of self-hatred cemented into the wall between God's heart and ours. Behind such stone walls, we cannot receive the love and acceptance God offers or direct a dark world to the joy and love of the heavenly Father. We cannot celebrate or share a love we refuse to receive.

Self—Hatred as Self—Absorption

I tremble to delve into this, reluctant to tell those of us who already struggle with self-rejection that we function in a sin we haven't recognized. But I must, because I know that without an essential repentance we cannot tear down this pernicious stone and put life-giving self-acceptance in its place.

We must face a hard truth: the stone of self-hatred cripples us so we hobble through life *self-absorbed*. Today many mistakenly think of self-hatred as humility, but they are incorrect; self-hatred is instead a painful manifestation of total self-orientation.

Think of the picture of the plant in the first chapter of this book. The plant has definite needs for life. When a stone wall obstructs the sunlight it requires, the plant twists itself to seek what it needs.

God created us with the need to drink in his love, accepting ourselves in light of his acceptance of us. When this happens, we become self-forgetful. With our needs met, we can move on, becoming more and more absorbed with God—his activity, his creations, and his people. When we block that love through failure to accept ourselves, our need does not go away; it goes underground.

We twist ourselves, attempting to fill our need for acceptance with achievements, people-pleasing, control, addictions, weight-loss, possessions, eating, romantic love, muscle-building, etc. But if we base our self-acceptance on anything other than our Father's love, our souls quake under the tenuousness of our value: physical attractiveness fades; possessions can be taken away; today's achievements are forgotten tomorrow; people are only sometimes pleased; the pleasure of drink, or drugs, or sex is fleeting. This base-level anxiety about our deepest needs keeps us self-focused—rather than God-focused.

What goes through our minds when we walk into a room full of people? When we live with self-rejection, it can take two forms and sometimes alternates back and forth: either we live in painful self-consciousness, or we defend ourselves against the rejection we expect by rejecting others preemptively. In the grip of self-consciousness we walk into the room thinking, "Who will I sit with? Do they want me here? Are they laughing at me? Do they think I'm fat? If I open my mouth, then they will know I am stupid."

Calloused by self-protection, "knowing" others will reject us, we walk into the room thinking, "Look at him. He thinks he is better than everyone else. She dresses like that just to get attention. Christians are so judgmental; that's why they look down on everyone."

Self-rejection can take one more form—the form of a mask, as we talked about in chapter three. In this case, we craft a not quite true version of ourselves and seek experiences to reinforce it. I mention it here to point out there is another way to walk into a room, by putting on our mask. Then we think, "I've been working out; I look good. I know I will impress them with what I have to say. I am an important part of this group." Even though we use positive self-talk in this instance, it still emanates from self-rejection because we use the affirmation of others or of ourselves to make ourselves feel better. Our self-acceptance does not flow from knowing God loves us; it comes from having polished a version of ourselves that works to get us what we think we need.

When the stone of self-hatred comes down, we can walk into a crowded room free from self-consciousness, anger, or self-absorption. We become God-absorbed, living with worship and joy, showing genuine interest in and love for others. Then we might walk into a room thinking, "Look how the sunlight streams through those windows. And look at all the people God is drawing to himself. Ah, see that mother attending to her baby. Thank you, Father, for giving her such love for that little one. That man looks lonely; I'll go say hello to him." Free from self, we see God's work all around and even participate with him.

I have a friend like this. In her eighties now, wrinkled and small, she lives at peace with herself and in love with Jesus. Her love of God and her joy in loving people draw me and many others to her. She is beautiful. When I was with her last, the verse that kept going through my mind was, "He must increase, but I must decrease" (John 3:30). My friend accepted herself, in light of God's love for her, long ago, and she spent her life getting to know Jesus instead of worrying about herself. Spending even an hour with her is life-giving.

Repenting of Self–Absorption

When we reject ourselves, we hold ourselves up against a standard, decide we do not measure up, and obsess over our shortcomings. We might despair and wallow in self-hatred, or we might work frantically at creating a mask that does meet the standard. Either way, we make an idol of ourselves. We want to be worthy of a form of self-worship, and we will not be content until…we lose twenty pounds, earn a certain income, live in that neighborhood, conquer this addiction, become a better parent, get that person to love us, etc. We hate or reject ourselves for not meeting these self-imposed standards.

Self-hatred is a terrible cycle of SELF: we make the standard; we measure ourselves; we judge ourselves; we reject ourselves; we work on ourselves. This is what Payne calls the "hell of self."[28] If we include God in this cycle at all, we see him as an extension of ourselves—a more angry, judgmental, and fearsome version of ourselves, who also rejects us.

Therefore, we take our first step toward self-acceptance, though it strikes us as counter-intuitive, when we confess and repent of self-absorption and self-hatred. The spiritual exercises at the end of this chapter will guide you in doing this if necessary.

Growing in Humility

This repentance grows us in true humility—self-acceptance. I hope you can see self-hatred is not humility, but a twisted form of pride. Humility tears down the stone of self-hatred by settling self-acceptance in its place. Whereas self-absorption requires no faith, the humility of self-acceptance requires deep trust in God. In humility we submit to being the person he created us to be, we affirm he did well in creating us, and we trust—even in our sin—he loves us because he is marvelously loving.

When repentance has developed humility in us, we stop obsessing about ourselves. We can say to God, "I will never measure up to my standards, let alone yours. But you love sinners. You love me and have rescued me from my failures, shortcomings, and sins by the death of your Son. I love you for being a merciful, rescuing God, and I accept myself because even though I am deeply fallen, I am loved by the most glorious Person in the universe."

When we embrace humility, the stone of self-hatred comes down, and the channels open between God's heart and our heart. We can soak up his love and grow in maturity. More and more we stop focusing on ourselves and fix our eyes on God. We accept ourselves and then forget ourselves—transfixed by the glory, love, and mercy of our good God. We become like my friend, whose life is fragrant with the fruit of living with the heart-posture "He must increase, but I must decrease." When we repent our self-absorbed self-hatred, we feel blessed to be LESS because he is MORE.

The Old Self and the New Self

Self-acceptance does not require us to like everything about ourselves. The Bible teaches we have an "old self"—related to the fallen world, resistant to God, and irredeemably tainted by sin. This old self must die, symbolized at baptism by our sinking under the water in identification with Jesus's death (Romans 6:3-4).

But the Bible also teaches in Christ we have a new self—a self created to reflect God's glory and live eternally with him. Our new self is symbolized at baptism by our being lifted out of the waters, identifying with Jesus in his resurrection (Ephesians 4:22-24; Romans 6:5-8).

Through self-acceptance we stop trying to fix up the old self and let it die, or put it to death, trusting the Father to recreate us into our new selves.

Words of Life

After we have repented of self-absorption and the twisted pride of self-hatred, we must have what we need for life—the love of our Father. At Jesus's baptism the Father speaks words of blessing and life over his Son: "You are my beloved Son; with you I am well pleased" (Mark 1:11).

Not long after, Jesus says to Satan, "Man shall not live by bread alone, but by every word that comes from the mouth of God" (Matthew 4:4). Jesus needed the loving words of his Father more than he needed bread. And we must have his words as well.

When we are in Christ, we are "in the Beloved" (Ephesians 1:6) and *that* is the transfixing joy and wonder of the gospel. God the Father's loving words are for us too. We learn to receive them through meditation on scripture and listening prayer. We heal into self-acceptance as we sit with God's words found in scripture and soak them into our hearts. And we also hear his life-giving words through listening prayer. The spiritual exercises that follow will help you receive God's love through his written words; they will also give you guidance to hear the life-giving words his Spirit speaks to you through listening prayer.

Identifying Self–Hatred

In preparation for the spiritual exercises, please take a look at the list below to discern if stones of self-hatred or self-rejection exist in the wall between God's heart and yours. Please read the list thoughtfully and mark any statements that describe your experience.

Symptoms of Self-Hatred or Self-Rejection

- Cursing at yourself in your head
- Saying bad things about yourself to yourself or others
- Bragging
- Discomfort with compliments
- Inordinate craving of compliments
- Mistrust of those who claim to love you
- Self-destructive behavior
- Addiction
- A sense, when you have sinned, of great shame and condemnation
- Envy or jealousy
- Intense self-consciousness or shyness
- A pervading sense of guilt or shame
- Perpetual criticism of your physical body
- Seeking out friendships or romantic relationships with

people who treat you poorly

- Being overly sensitive to criticism
- Terror of rejection
- Perfectionism
- Depression
- Paralysis in the face of decisions
- Fear of taking risks

If you recognize any of these tendencies in yourself, stones of self-hatred or self-rejection may be walling off your heart from the joy of self-acceptance in light of God's love for you. I pray you will move prayerfully through the following spiritual exercises and find grace to tear down these stones and accept yourself as God's beloved. The world aches for the gifts only you can give us.

Spiritual Exercises for Chapter Seven

A Daily Prayer for Those Who Struggle with Self-Acceptance

1. Pray this prayer from Ephesians for yourself today and every day as long as you seek self-acceptance:

    I pray that out of his glorious riches he may strengthen you with power through his Spirit in your inner being, so that Christ may dwell in your hearts through faith. And I pray that you, being rooted and established in love, may have power, together with all the Lord's holy people, to grasp how wide and long and high and deep is the love of Christ, and to know this love that surpasses knowledge—that you may be filled to the measure of all the fullness of God (Ephesians 3:16-19 NIV).

2. If any strong feelings—doubts, anxieties, frustrations, fears, or joys—come to mind while you pray this prayer, take time to tell God about those feelings. Ask him if he has anything he wants to say to you about them. Record what you hear in your journal.

Discerning the Roots of Self-Hatred

1. If you struggle with self-acceptance, you have found some parts of yourself too shameful or sinful for even God's forgiving love. Ask the Lord to reveal to you the places in your heart where this is happening. What is it you believe God will find unacceptable or unforgivable? Tell God about these things, or write them in your journal.

2. Is there a person who communicated these lies to you, either directly or indirectly? If you are able, forgive this person, using the prayers provided in the chapter on extending forgiveness.

3. Make Psalm 51:1-13 your prayer.

4. See yourself before the cross and confess your "unforgivable" sins or shortcomings to him there. Release these things to him and see them enter his body on the cross.

5. Now pray 1 John 1:9: "If we confess our sins, he is faithful and just to forgive us our sins and to cleanse us from all unrighteousness." Receive God's forgiveness in prayer.

Renouncing Self-Hatred

1. If you have lived hating yourself, then you have lived in sin against yourself and against God, who created you and loves you. You have lived in self-absorption, thinking that if only you didn't have this or that sin or problem or shortcoming, he would love you. And you have rejected his provision for your iniquity—the blood of his Son, Jesus. Ask God if this is true of you.

2. If you discover you have sinned in this way, confess and renounce this sin through prayer. Start today and pray for as many days as necessary until the power of self-rejection is broken. If you are struggling with how to pray, then you may find the following prayer helpful:

    Father in heaven, creator and sustainer of my life (Colossians 1:16-17), and the One who gave up his Son for me (Galatians 2:20), I confess I have hated myself. I have stood in judgment over myself and have condemned and rejected myself. I confess

118

the self-absorption behind this self-condemnation and my rejection of your provision for my sin (Isaiah 53:6). Today I renounce self-hatred, self-condemnation, and self-rejection. I reject any lies I have believed from the enemy of my soul, who is a liar and the father of lies (John 8:44), regarding my unworthiness to be accepted by God. I believe I am loved by the Father of lights, who in love chose me before the foundation of the world, that I should be holy and blameless before him (James 1:17; Ephesians 1:4). The shed blood of Jesus covers all of my sin, the sins of my past, the sins of today that I am not even aware of, and the sins I will commit in the days before he brings me home. There is no condemnation for me because I am found in Christ Jesus (Romans 8:1). I commit myself to regard myself as Christ regards me—as deeply fallen, and deeply loved, as rescued, redeemed, and restored through the great mercy of my God. I commit to stop rejecting myself, hating myself, and standing in condemnation over myself. I confess the folly and pride of such a practice, and I renounce it here today. I ask you, Holy Spirit, to fill me to the measure of all the fullness of God and to make me able to know the love of Christ for me that surpasses knowledge (Ephesians 3:19) that I may spread everywhere the fragrance of the knowledge of him (2 Corinthians 2:14).

Knowing God's Love through Scripture

1. Our self-acceptance flows from understanding God loves and accepts us. Pray every day and as often as it comes to

mind, asking God to help you to know his love for you.

2. Meditation upon scripture can help us learn God's love for us. I have given you two scriptures below to begin with. Read these passages slowly and prayerfully as many times as your heart desires. Journal any phrases that stand out to you and write your thoughts about these words. Turn these words and your responses into prayers to your Father.

- Ephesians 5:25-27

- Zephaniah 3:16-17

Five: Knowing God's Love through Listening Prayer

1. Turn these words into a prayer: "Let me hear in the morning of your steadfast love, for in you I trust" (Psalm 143:8).

2. Quiet yourself in the presence of the Lord.

3. Make Samuel's words your prayer, "Speak, for your servant hears" (1 Samuel 3:10).

4. Listen in quietness for anything the Lord would say to you.

5. Journal anything you believe you hear from him.

6. Respond to him in prayer, thanking him for his words of life.

Note: Learning to listen to the Lord this way can take practice. Please don't be discouraged if you hear nothing. Sometimes he asks us to simply sit in his presence, and that is healing in itself. Also, the Lord will never speak a word that is contrary to scripture. If you hear things that confuse you, please seek the counsel of a wise friend or mentor to discern what you hear.

Discussion Questions for Chapter Seven:
The Stone of Self–Hatred

1. What is your experience with what Charles Kraft calls "Worm Theologies"?

2. How have you seen false humility being taught as Christian maturity?

3. To what degree are you able to agree with Jasona about self-acceptance as an essential Christian virtue?

4. Have you experienced the an loving someone who refuses to accept himself or herself? Please explain.

5. How is someone who has not accepted himself or herself self-absorbed? To what degree does this seem counter-intuitive to you?

6. Have you been blessed to know someone who has accepted himself or herself in the light of God's love? What was this experience like?

7. Where do you find yourself on the path to self-acceptance?

Chapter Eight
The Stone of Demonic Oppression

*"The reason the Son of God appeared was to
destroy the works of the devil."*
~ 1 John 3:8

*"Be strong in the Lord and in the strength
of his might. Put on the whole armor of God,
that you may be able to stand against
the schemes of the devil."*
~ Ephesians 6:10-11

The summer I turned eighteen I did two contradictory things.
I read C.S. Lewis's *Mere Christianity* and understood it was
true. And I read books on astrology and meditation and recited a
mantra—a mysterious phrase I found in one of the books—over
and over to give me spiritual insight or peace.

I left for college that fall eager for "fun" and "freedom," but
I sensed God compelling me to seek him. Disgruntled, I joined
an Intervarsity Christian Fellowship Bible study; I did not want
to discuss "religion" while everyone else partied. But a few
weeks into the fall semester everything changed.

I lay in bed late one night, easing into sleep, thinking of
friends, school assignments, and rowing. Then—suddenly—a
news report I had long forgotten stabbed into my mind and
jolted me awake. I stared wide-eyed into the dark with my heart
pounding. The horror of the story—a teenage girl abducted by a

man who raped her, cut off her arms at her elbows, and left her to die—consumed me. I thought I might be losing my mind. I trembled with dread and finally had to tiptoe down the hall to the bathroom where I could turn on the lights, breathe in and out, and try to regain a sense of normality.

My fall semester turned—overnight—into a season of unrelenting terror. Every day I heard another story of torture, abuse, rape, or calamity, and I reeled internally, wondering how to live in a world where such things happen. In an inexplicable instant life had changed for me into a nightmare I couldn't wake up from; my dread of evil eclipsed all the good in the world. When I wasn't drowning in fear, shameful thoughts intruded into my mind and filled me with self-loathing.

Finally, I met with a pastor who confirmed what I intuited, that I was in a battle with evil—though I had never heard of spiritual warfare. He taught me to fight. He showed me I could command demons to leave me alone whenever fears or unwanted thoughts assailed me. I fought for freedom, and I experienced relief. I became able to hear about evil without being swallowed by terror, and I could delight in goodness, beauty, and joy again.

My relationship with the Lord transformed from reluctance to passion. As he restored me, I understood I would live as a committed Christian woman—a new paradigm for me. I had planned to be an actress or reporter, living the life I admired in magazines. I hadn't grown up in church, and until then I had lacked even the awareness that some people considered themselves Christians. But I knew I needed God—desperately—and I owed him my life.

I now understand I had unwittingly opened the doors of my soul to demonic oppression through the occult practices of reciting a mantra and exploring astrology. And I thank God for using my foolishness, and the resulting torment, to draw me to himself. I wish it hadn't required such suffering for me to come to him, but I wouldn't trade it. I hope this encourages you that if you have struggled against evil, God can use even this for your good, just as he promises: "For those who love God all things work together for good" (Romans 8:28).

The prayers and counsel of that wise pastor helped me tremendously—the intense and terrorizing attacks ended. However, it was another twenty-five years before I found fuller freedom from fear and guilt that oppressed me in quieter, but still crippling, ways.

I don't want it to take that long for you. Because of the Lord's kindness, I have learned much since then, and I have experienced a freedom I never imagined possible. Now I want to equip you to understand the ways your enemy may have forged heavy stones of demonic oppression to keep your heart walled off from God's heart. I want you to find freedom too. I do not want you to be "outwitted by Satan" or "ignorant of his designs" (2 Corinthians 2:11) as I was.

We Have an Enemy and We Are in a Battle

Our enemy slithers into our story in the third chapter of Genesis. Most scholars believe he was one of God's most powerful angels who grew jealous of God and led a rebellion, leading to his expulsion from heaven along with the angels who sinned with him (Luke 10:18; Isaiah 14:12-15). He is now the chief of the fallen angels (demons) and has set himself against God and those who bear God's image—men and women.

We must never mistakenly think that Satan's power and influence compare to God's. Satan is not the "opposite" of God. He is a created being in rebellion against God. His days are numbered. At the judgment he will be "thrown into the lake of fire and sulfur" (Revelation 20:10).

But for now he strikes at God's heart by assailing God's beloved—mankind. When Satan seduced Adam and Eve to rebel against God, he was able to usher in death, chaos, natural disasters, and every type of evil we suffer on earth. Hunger, war, death, aging, oppression, abuse, torture, terrorism, mental illness, divorce, abortion, disease, cancer—everything that destroys life and opposes the good and beautiful purposes of God's kingdom—results from the tragic alliance mankind made with God's enemy at the Fall.

Jesus's incarnation announced the beginning of the end of Satan's reign of terror: God's Son came to undo the work of the enemy and restore the rule of God. He reversed diseases, raised the dead, encouraged the poor, and forgave sinners—proclaiming the arrival of the kingdom of God (Mark 1:15). Peter summarizes the ministry of Jesus like this: "God anointed Jesus of Nazareth with the Holy Spirit and with power. He went about doing good and healing all who were oppressed by the devil, for God was with him" (Acts 10:38). And Paul describes salvation like this: "He has delivered us from the domain of darkness and transferred us to the kingdom of his beloved Son" (Colossians 1:13).

Since Jesus's resurrection, Satan's time grows shorter and shorter. Knowing this increases his fury: "Woe to you, O earth and sea, for the devil has come down to you in great wrath, because he knows that his time is short!" (Revelation 12:12). Until Jesus comes a second time to destroy the influence of the enemy forever, we suffer this "wrath" of the devil. Jesus calls him "the ruler of this world" (John 12:31), and you only need to open your morning newspaper to get some idea of what he is up to.

On a widespread level he entices rulers to injustice, kindles war, fuels destructive ideologies, deceives anyone he can, and promotes degrading and sinful values. He oppresses us personally by hurling flaming arrows of temptation or doubt at us (Ephesians 6:16), seeking to devour us like a prowling lion (1 Peter 5:8), wrestling with us (Ephesians 6:12), sending people to persecute or attack us (John 8:40-41, 44), lying to us (John 8:44), and accusing us (Revelation 12:10). His attacks are intense, personal, and threatening. The biblical writers exhort us—in the face of this onslaught—to wise, courageous, and enduring resistance. I want to equip you to resist.

Areas of Particular Vulnerability

We are aided in resisting and overcome the assaults of our enemy if we understand some things that make us especially vulnerable to his attacks and oppression.[29]

Persistent Sin

Paul warns, "Do not let the sun go down while you are still angry, and do not give the devil a foothold" (Ephesians 4:26-27 NIV). Hanging on to anger gives the devil the opportunity to oppress us. This is true of many types of sin: control, pride, violence, resentment, gossip, addiction, greed, etc. When we indulge, over and over, in the same sin, we may end up oppressed by a spirit associated with that sin. The demon then super-charges our temptation. Larry's story exemplifies the way this kind of spirit operates.

Larry grew up in a perfect storm for oppression by a spirit of lust: His mother was emotionally unavailable to him; his family had a history of addiction and sexual promiscuity; and a family member exposed Larry to pornography when he was very young. By the time Larry was in high school he used pornography daily.

When Larry reached adulthood he fought to overcome his addiction. He committed his life to the Lord and stopped looking at pornography. Still, he struggled every day with what he described as "lust on steroids." Even after Larry married he was wracked with lust—looking for a woman who would fill the hole inside of him—and struggled with anger toward his new wife for "not being enough."

Finally, at his request, people prayed for Larry and commanded spirits of lust to leave. Larry's life was changed. The
super-charged nature of his temptation was broken. He didn't
feel overpowered by lust any longer. He could resist "normal
amounts of temptation with normal amounts of will-power and
prayer." Over time the temptation lessened and his love for his
wife blossomed.

If you identify with Larry's story, you will find help in the
spiritual exercises related to sin at the end of this chapter.

Trauma

In the area of trauma, we see the cruelty of our enemy. Like
a wolf stalking the limping foal at the back of the herd, he
pounces on us when we are wounded. Weak and bleeding, we
can do little to kick him off. Digging his claws into our back, he
tells us lies: You deserved this; it's your fault; God failed you.
In these cases, our wounds make us vulnerable to oppression
by spirits of guilt, shame, fear, or anxiety.

About two years ago, the Lord freed me from demonic
oppression related to trauma. Doug and I were offered a trip
to Spain, but I was terrified something bad would happen to
my kids while we were gone. I felt so ashamed that I *could not*
trust God to take care of my children. I confessed to a friend,
"It hurts to be this afraid."

I asked the Lord about my fear and pain, and he showed me
I blamed myself for my accident: I did something stupid—sat
in the open hatch—so I suffered. I lived in fear, waiting for
the next time I would do something selfish or stupid, like go
to Spain with my husband, when my *children* would suffer for
my mistake.

He also showed me a picture of myself with an evil, black
chain circling my neck. It was so heavy I felt it suffocating me.
I sensed God's Spirit telling me it was a "chain of trauma"—all

the traumatic events of my childhood forged together into this crushing weight.

"Help!" I cried to the Lord, and I heard him say, "I want your friends to help you." I made an appointment for myself with the Intensive Healing Prayer team at our church. In our time of prayer, I saw the evil, heavy chain weighing me down, but one of our prayer ministers discerned more than one thing hung around my neck. She asked me to hand each one to Jesus. I saw Jesus in my mind, and I reached to lift one of the "chains," but my hand grasped instead a snake called "Guilt." I gave it to Jesus and he threw it into the water of the harbor at Tokeen (where my accident happened). It sank and drowned.

Jesus then took upon himself my heavy chain of trauma and gave me instead a garland of flowers. I felt a new ability to grow in trusting God with my children, and I happily planned the trip to Spain. (Imagine how delighted Doug was!) A spirit of guilt, using the trauma of my accident as a foothold, oppressed my ability to trust the Lord's promises of care and protection. Jesus freed me from that oppression. Thank you, Jesus.

I hope you are encouraged reading this that sometimes when we don't know how or can't fight for ourselves, we can ask the Lord for help and he steps in and rescues us. If you have trauma in your story, and suffer from things such as I describe here, the spiritual exercises at the end of this chapter will help you fight and seek him for rescue.

Occult Sin

Ann came to talk to me about receiving prayer. During our conversation, we began to discuss her addiction to horror movies, and she became nauseated and nearly threw up. I prayed for the Lord to help her and commanded demons to stop bothering her, and she was able to continue talking with me. She told me about her deep involvement in occult activities: séances, casting spells and curses, seeking healing from spiritualists, studying witchcraft, wearing amulets, attempting table-lifting, and using a Ouija board.

Occult activities encompass any avenue we use to seek knowledge or spiritual power other than through the Holy Spirit. The Holy Spirit provides the only safe door to the spiritual realm. Using any other entry point gives the demonic the opportunity to oppress us, as I described in my story at the beginning of this chapter.

Ann had unintentionally invited demonic oppression and suffered terrible repercussions: anxiety, depression, suicidal thoughts, health problems, headaches, and self-loathing. As she and I spoke of her desire to be free, the demons afflicted her with nausea to interrupt our conversation and frighten her into ceasing to seek help.

In fact Ann did, without explanation, stop coming for prayer. I feel sad when I think of her because I saw in her the strength, beauty, intelligence, and passion to tell others about the Lord that characterize a woman God has gifted for leadership. The spirits that oppress her keep one of God's leaders in a nearly suicidal state of depression, anxiety, and self-hatred by super-charging her addictions and filling her soul with lies about herself. I pray for Ann, that the Lord blesses her with complete freedom from this demonic bondage.

Susan did continue to come for prayer. Her obsession with finding out the future led her to try voodoo, psychic hotlines, and fortune-telling. But seeking knowledge from the occult provided a foothold for oppression. She suffered from depression and anxiety and had attempted suicide several times.

The prayer ministers commanded the demons oppressing her to leave. They addressed shame, false guilt, death, divination, and witchcraft. She left us a celebratory voice message some time later, saying she could smile for the first time in so long. Thank God!

Occult spirits can be powerful and dangerous. In our ministry we have encountered some with names like "Oppressor" or "Death." If you know you have been deeply involved in occult activities, I encourage you to seek prayer from those experienced in praying for deliverance from evil spirits.

How Do We Know If We Have Stones of Demonic Oppression?

I understand this can be an uncomfortable topic. I felt terrified and ashamed the first time someone suggested I might be oppressed by a demon. But God has compassion for our oppression. Jesus describes us as "harassed and helpless, like sheep without a shepherd" (Matthew 9:36). In Psalm 18:17-19, David describes God coming to his rescue: "He rescued me from my strong enemy and from those who hated me, for they were too mighty for me. They confronted me in the day of my calamity, but the Lord was my support. He brought me out into a broad place; he rescued me, because he delighted in me."

Loved ones, Jesus came to heal us from Satan's oppression. We may feel shame or fear when we think about seeking freedom because the spirits oppressing us want us to think they are not real, we are bad or dirty, and God could not love us.

Please don't listen to the lies. Take courage.

God loves you more than you know, calls you to more than you can imagine, and offers you freedom. When he removes stones of demonic oppression, the truth about the glory of God's love will reach your heart.

Sometimes we know we are in a battle with evil. I did, even though I didn't have any categories for thinking about it. Other times, we need the Holy Spirit to wake us up to the oppression and stir us to resist.

Satan and his demons endeavor to keep us from God's heart and prevent us from trusting him, loving him, and serving him joyfully. They want us to think of ourselves as low, dirty, and unworthy and to think of God as distant, angry, or nonexistent. They try to enslave us in sin and use us to hurt other people.

When they are achieving these goals, we suffer in common and somewhat predictable ways, even though we feel as though we are the only ones going through these difficulties. Please prayerfully consider whether you live with any of these symptoms of demonic oppression:

- Accusatory thoughts
- Hearing voices
- Frightening night disturbances
- Addiction
- Fascination with evil
- Intense fear, anxiety, or shame
- Defeat in sin
- Obsessive thoughts of suicide or murder
- Difficulty praying, reading scripture, or worshiping
- Difficulty receiving communion
- Psychic powers
- Uncontrollable cursing in your head
- Intense anger or rage
- Blasphemous or unwanted thoughts
- Self-hatred
- Racism, prejudice, or hatred toward another group of people

- Profound discouragement or emotional paralysis
- Inability to believe God loves you

It is possible to experience any of these symptoms and not be undergoing demonic oppression. However, if you suffer from a number of these symptoms, or one of them intensely, you may find help in the spiritual exercises at the end of this chapter. Be encouraged. I wrote these verses on a notecard I kept in my pocket during the time I was under attack:

Your adversary the devil prowls around like a roaring lion, seeking someone to devour. Resist him, firm in your faith, knowing that the same kinds of suffering are being experienced by your brotherhood throughout the world. And after you have suffered a little while, the God of all grace, who has called you to his eternal glory in Christ, will himself restore, confirm, strengthen, and establish you (1 Peter 5:8-10).

These promises proved true for me, and I trust God's restoration waits just around the corner for you.

How Do We Overcome Demonic Oppression?

God promises us strength to fight our enemies. Paul says, "Be strong in the Lord and in the strength of his might. Put on the whole armor of God, that you may be able to stand against the schemes of the devil" (Ephesians 6:10-11). And Paul tells us about our armor: truth, righteousness, readiness to share God's good news, faith, salvation, God's word, and prayer (Ephesians 6:14-18). Dressed in God's spiritual protection, we are ready to fight.

When I first began to pray Ephesians 6, I thought I put on God's armor by saying the words, "I put on the breastplate of righteousness. I put on the helmet of salvation." But this is a superficial interpretation. Now I read these verses understanding Paul calls us to *a way of life* that arms us.

God's word is our sword, its truth our belt. Just as a fencer or sword-fighter ceaselessly practices thrusts and jabs, strengthening his muscles and sharpening his reflexes for an anticipated match, we train ourselves with God's truth in the scriptures so we can wield it effectively. Jesus fights Satan's temptations in the wilderness this way. Each time Satan entices Jesus with a different reward—relief from hunger (Matthew 4:3), instant fame (Matthew 4:5-6), power (Matthew 4:8-9)—Jesus defeats temptation by quoting Deuteronomy aloud: "Man shall not live by bread alone, but by every word that comes from the mouth of God" (Matthew 4:4); "You shall not put the Lord your God to the test" (Matthew 4:7); and "You shall worship the Lord your God and him only shall you serve" (Matthew 4:10). Picture Jesus as a brilliant, well-practiced, sword-fighter, who—even in extreme exhaustion—skillfully deflects the assaults of his enemy.

Paul says righteousness—right living before God—is our breastplate, a covering to protect our heart and other vital organs. He means we prepare for success in battle by surrendering every area of our life to God, repenting of all known sin. He also means Jesus's righteousness protects us. And faith in our loving God and his Son is our shield.

Paul says we are to put on our feet "the readiness given by the gospel of peace" (Ephesians 6:15). We don't just stop sinning, we strap on our "running shoes," readying ourselves to do anything God asks. Like runners on the starting line eager to hear "Go!" we say to God, "What have you got for me today?" Our willing, eager obedience protects us from being dragged aside by our enemy.

Prayer arms us and those we love. Paul exhorts us to pray "at all times in the Spirit, with all prayer and supplication...

making supplication for all the saints" (Ephesians 6:18). When the enemy attacks, we cry to God for help. The psalmist says, "Out of my distress I called on the Lord; the Lord answered me and set me free" (Psalm 118:5).

So we defend ourselves from our enemy, primarily, by choosing ways of living that protect and arm us: soaking in God's words, devoting ourselves to prayer, surrendering sinful patterns, exercising faith, and readying ourselves for eager obedience. Then, fully armed, we are ready to fight.

James says, "Submit yourselves therefore to God. Resist the devil, and he will flee from you" (James 4:7). The armor-of-God way of life correlates with James's first command: submit. Now I want to talk about the second command: resist.

Sometimes we apply ourselves to the things Paul teaches, but nothing gets better. We continue feeling depressed. The accusing thoughts remain. We still hate ourselves. This was true of me my freshman year of college. When the battle against me got so heated, I did surrender myself to God as best I knew how: I stopped partying, joined a Bible study, prayed, and read my Bible. But I didn't feel better.

I had to learn to fight—to resist—to command demons to leave me alone.

Preparing to Fight

Once we have chosen the armor-of-God way of life, we only need to take three preparatory steps before we command oppressive demons to leave us alone: repentance, renunciation, and request.

Repentance
Repentance is a beautiful and powerful posture of the human heart. When we repent we tell the Lord about our sorrow over our sin and our desire to turn from it and live in step with his

Spirit. God will not turn his back on a repentant soul. James says, "God opposes the proud, but gives grace to the humble" (James 4:6). He says this *right before* he promises if we resist the devil he will flee from us! (James 4:7). When we humble ourselves in repentance, the grace of God floods to meet us and we have strength to send our enemies away.

Renunciation

We renounce something when we formally and audibly declare our rejection of it and our refusal to go along with it any longer. We can renounce sin patterns, believing our enemy's lies, or occult practices. Such renunciations weaken our enemy's footholds.

Request

Before we command spirits to leave us alone, we ask the Lord to renew us in his Holy Spirit, grant us his authority, protect us and those we love, and help us in the battle. We join the psalmist who cries to God when his enemies buzz around him like bees: "Save us, we pray, O Lord! O Lord, we pray, give us success!" (Psalm 118:25).

Resisting Our Enemy

In the gospels Jesus speaks aloud to demons, rebuking them, and commanding them to stop harassing people. He says to the demon oppressing a man in a synagogue, "Be silent, and come out of him!" (Mark 1:25). And he says to the unclean spirit oppressing a young boy, "You mute and deaf spirit, I command you, come out of him and never enter him again" (Mark 9:25). The unclean spirits obey him.

Paul uses the same approach. A girl with a demon follows Paul and Silas everywhere, disrupting their work by shouting about them. Finally Paul, "having become greatly annoyed, turned and said to the spirit, 'I command you in the name of

Jesus Christ to come out of her.' And it came out that very hour"
(Acts 16:18).

Jesus has authority over demons (Mark 1:27). And Jesus, by
the Holy Spirit, lives in us (Colossians 1:27). So we, like Paul,
can take up the authority of Jesus in us and command evil spirits
to leave us alone. We can say, "In the name of Jesus, leave, and
never come back!" We can rebuke them with scripture as well.
We do this aloud—in a firm voice.

As I was becoming free from torment, I spoke out, rebuking
the spirits attacking me with words like "greater is he who lives
in me than he who lives in the world," which I took from 1 John
4:4. I also audibly lifted the shield of faith: I said, "I am a child
of the living God, purchased by the shed blood of Jesus. You
have no right to touch me!" And the attacks abated.

Sometimes we find additional power to fight and resist
when we name the spirit bothering us—as Jesus did when he
addressed the deaf/mute spirit. We can ask the Lord to reveal
to us a name if he will. We can also take a guess; if we struggle
with sin, we can say, "In the name of Jesus, I command any
spirit of _____ (*name the sin*) oppressing me to leave me.
Now!" We can do the same with guilt, fear, shame, etc.

Be Courageous

As you pray through the spiritual exercises for this chapter,
I pray you will have courage. God is with you, and his power
far surpasses that of our enemy: "Be strong and courageous. Do
not be frightened, and do not be dismayed, for the Lord your
God is with you wherever you go" (Joshua 1:9). God wants to
help you tear down any stones of demonic oppression standing
between him and you. When these stones fall, his mighty love
and delight in you—exactly what your enemy wants to prevent
you from discovering—will make you alive like never before.
Please don't give up.

Spiritual Exercises for Chapter Eight

Remembering the One Who Saves You

1. Prayerfully read through Psalm 18:1-19 and 31-39. Turn the pleas into your cries to the Lord. Turn the promises into prayers. Praise the Lord for who he is and who he promises to be to you.

Lord, Do I Need You to Free Me from My Enemies?

1. Read Psalm 139:1-6, 11-12, and 23-24. Make verses 23 and 24 your prayer to the Lord. Please read once again through the list of symptoms of demonic oppression listed in this chapter, asking the Lord to show you if evil spirits are harassing you. Journal anything he shows you.

Identifying Vulnerabilities

1. If you suspect you suffer from demonic oppression, you will be aided in your journey to freedom by discerning if the enemy is taking advantage of any particular area of vulnerability. Please prayerfully consider whether you might be vulnerable in any of these areas:

Trauma

If your struggles have to do with anxiety, rejection, fear, or shame, the roots of your oppression may lie in trauma. The Lord remembers every moment of your life. Ask him to show you the roots of your struggle. If something comes to mind, turn to the chapter on unhealed memories and work through the exercises provided. Make Psalm 23:3, "He restores my soul," your prayer. After praying for healing of the roots of your trauma, you can move to the "Resist" prayers below and command any spirit that has used your trauma to oppress you to leave you alone.

Sin

If you wrestle with a sin you cannot overcome, a temptation that feels "super-charged," then you may struggle against a spirit of sin. Ask yourself, "Do I desire to be free of this sin?" If you cannot honestly say you desire freedom, ask the Lord to give you this desire. Ask him to show you why he would be so serious about sin that he would say, "If your right eye causes you to sin, tear it out and throw it away" (Matthew 5:29). When you are ready, you may adapt the "Repent, Renounce, Request, and Resist" prayers to your situation.

Occult

"There shall not be found among you anyone who burns his son or his daughter as an offering, anyone who practices divination or tells fortunes or interprets omens, or a sorcerer or a charmer or a medium or a necromancer or one who inquires of the dead" (Deuteronomy 18:10-11). Ask the Lord to bring to your mind any occult practice you have participated in. Modern-day expressions include following horoscopes, using Ouija boards, seeing fortune-tellers or palm readers, meditative chanting, or watching horror movies.

If you suspect your struggle may be with occult spirits, you must get rid of any occult objects. Please destroy them. Then pray the following prayers, or similar prayers that come from your heart.

Four: Preparing for the Fight

Before you command the enemy to leave you alone, please pray through these prayers of repentance, renunciation, and request. I wrote the prayer of repentance for repenting of sin, and the prayer of renunciation for renouncing occult activity, but please adapt them according to your situation. Also, if you need to repent of occult activity or sin, please ask the Lord who he would like you to tell about this. Commit to telling this person soon, or seek them out to tell them now. The Lord says to "confess your sins to one another and pray for one another, that you may be healed" (James 5:16). When we confess to each other and pray for each other we find healing and freedom more quickly than when we pray alone.

- **Repent:** "Lord Jesus, I acknowledge before you that I have sinned by _____. Over and over I have chosen this sinful way of trying to get the needs of my heart met. I am sorry for not trusting you and for choosing this sin. Please forgive me. And please fill me anew with your Holy Spirit, cleanse me of this sin, and grant me power to resist temptation. Rescue me from my enemies, be my God of peace, and sanctify me completely so that my whole spirit, soul, and body will be kept blameless at your coming, my Lord Jesus Christ. Amen" (1 Thessalonians 5:23).

- **Renounce:** "In the name of Jesus Christ, I renounce all occult involvement and activity. I renounce_____ (*name the practices you have engaged in*). I reject all forms of spiritual power other than the Holy Spirit of the Living God. I renounce and break any invitation or allegiance I have made, knowingly or unknowingly, to demonic forces of evil. I bring myself under the shed blood of Jesus Christ and submit myself to his authority alone."

- **Request:** "Lord Jesus, you are my strength, and I love you. Please be my rock, my fortress, and my deliverer. You are my God in whom I take refuge. I call upon you to save me from my strong enemy and from those who hate me, for they are too mighty for me. Thank you that you will rescue me because you delight in me (Psalm 18). Lord, please grant me your authority over the forces of evil. Please protect me and everyone I love from the evil one by the power of your name (John 17:11, NIV).

Resist the Enemy

Adapt this prayer according to your circumstances. You may address a spirit of sin, as the prayer is written, or you may change the prayer to address spirits of occult or trauma.

- **Resist:** Speak the following words aloud, with conviction: "In the name of Jesus Christ, by the authority granted to me through his death on the cross and his resurrection, and by the power of his Holy Spirit, I command any spirit of sin, particularly the sin of _____ to leave—now—and go to Jesus. I cancel your assignment against me. I break and renounce any alliance I ever made with you. I bring the shed blood of Jesus Christ between myself and any foul spirit. Greater is he who lives in me than he who lives in this world. I bring myself under the authority of Jesus and I command you to go."

You may need to speak these words, or similar ones, more than once. Repeat them any time in future days or weeks if you experience attack.

Resisting Fiery Darts

1. Read Ephesians 6:16: "In all circumstances take up the shield of faith, with which you can extinguish all the flaming darts of the evil one." If you cannot discern an area of vulnerability related to the attack you are suffering, and it feels like it is coming "out of the blue," raise your shield of faith—trust in God's promises to save you, cleanse you, and prepare a place for you in his kingdom. Then command any evil spirit sent to harass you to go to Jesus, adapting the prayer above, found under "Resist" to your circumstances. If you get no relief, ask someone else to pray with you or for you.

A Final Note: If you get no relief immediately, do not lose heart. Keep fighting! Sometimes freedom comes incrementally. But if, after sufficient time, you discern these types of prayers are not helping at all, please remember that many of our difficulties are not demonic. You can be assured you have explored the possibility that your difficulties come from spiritual attack and move on to consider other sources of relief for your suffering. If this is where you are, I am sorry you are hurting, and I pray you will find help—if not in a different chapter of this book—then through a source the Lord will provide.

You may pray this prayer for illumination: "Lord Jesus, I bring you my difficulties and pain. I believe you have confirmed to me that these troubles do not stem from demonic oppression. I ask you to be my great counselor and to send your Holy Spirit to help me. Please work in my heart and mind and through every circumstance and relationship in my life to bring me to freedom and joy. Help me be attentive to your leading and your invitations to wholeness. And give me faith to pursue any avenue of healing you show me. Amen."

Discussion Questions for Chapter Eight:
The Stone of Demonic Oppression

1. Jasona begins the chapter describing how God can take something evil and use even that for his good purposes. Have you experienced this in your life?

2. What has been your experience with spiritual warfare? Is this a new concept for you?

3. Have you encountered the idea that God and Satan are opposites? How would you describe them after reading this chapter?

4. Jasona talks about Satan's general attacks against groups or humankind and his specific attacks against individuals. Where do you think you can see some of his general attacks happening?

5. Discuss the teaching regarding different vulnerabilities for demonic oppression. Do you have questions or thoughts regarding this teaching? Did you discover any possible oppression happening in your life?

6. Describe your experience of praying the prayers Jasona provided in the spiritual exercises.

Chapter Nine
The Stone of Family Sin

"I am writing to you, fathers,
because you know him who is from the beginning.
I am writing to you, young men,
because you have overcome the evil one."
~ 1 John 2:13

"You were ransomed from the futile ways
inherited from your forefathers."
~ 1 Peter 1:18

Do you know the son of an alcoholic father who swore he would never be like his dad but now ruins his life with drink? Or do you know a woman with an abusive husband who also suffered as a child because her mother married a series of abusers?

Have you watched this tragic repetition in disbelief?

We assume that children who suffer from their parents' poor choices will not repeat their parents' mistakes, but truth defies logic. In family after family destructive patterns of addiction, abuse, divorce, workaholism, teen pregnancy, legalism, and prejudice roll through the generations. Why?

The answer is mysterious. But I have a hopeful message to share with you: Jesus wants to free us from the destructive patterns of sin operating in our families. I want to help you become aware of any such stone blocking your heart from soaking up God's healing love, to encourage you that Jesus can transform patterns of defeat in your family into streams of life, and to provide you with sample prayers and exercises to begin to combat any sin or possible oppression that may have come to you through your family.

I also hope to inspire you to pay attention to the ways Jesus has broken into your family system by reversing damaging patterns, redeeming hurts and losses, and growing new legacies of life. I hope you will find joy and thanksgiving welling up in you as you slow down to marvel at his artistry in your family tree.

My Family

In in my family tree, as in every other, branches of death twist and twine with branches of life.

My grandpa had six brothers. Every one of them died before they reached sixty-five—from heart attacks, cancer, a gun-shot wound, and influenza. My grandpa's brothers had three sons, and those young men died in a shooting incident, a boating accident, and a motorcycle accident before they were twenty-five. When my grandma died of cancer in her early fifties, my grandpa moved to his boat, drank a fifth of whiskey every day, and expected to die.

But he didn't.

He lived another twenty-four years and made peace with God before he died at age eighty-four. Somewhere in those years, I remember hearing him marvel he must be alive because of his family's prayers. Jesus had broken into his family tree and Grandpa knew many of us prayed for him often. *His* three sons, three grandsons, and one great-grandson are all living.

I rejoice because God interrupted a cycle of early male deaths in my family tree.

My great-grandmother's father loved Jesus. My family tells the story that his wife couldn't keep a coat on him because every time she gave him a new one he gave it away to people he met while he was street preaching.

My great-grandmother loved Jesus too and prayed for her family. She had a practice of writing people encouraging notes with scripture verses in them. When I got hurt on the boat, her church prayed night and day for me, holding twenty-four-hour prayer vigils during the weeks after my head injury. I believe my attending the Sunday school class in Petersburg and inviting Jesus into my heart a year later was a direct answer to their prayers for me.

A Biblical Understanding of Family Sin

You may have heard of the Bible's teaching about reaping and sowing: What we sow, we reap. Paul explains it this way: "Do not be deceived: God is not mocked, for whatever one sows, that will he also reap. For the one who sows to his own flesh will from the flesh reap corruption, but the one who sows to the Spirit will from the Spirit reap eternal life" (Galatians 6:7-8).

But perhaps you haven't heard of this related teaching: What our forefathers sowed, we reap. When the Lord gave Moses the ten commandments he said, "I the Lord your God am a jealous God, visiting the iniquity of the fathers on the children to the third and the fourth generation of those who hate me, but showing steadfast love to thousands of those who love me and keep my commandments" (Exodus 20:5-6).

The full meaning of these verses is difficult to grasp. That God is jealous does not mean he is petty, but that he is passionate about keeping his children near him. Somehow, the way sin— and God's steadfast love—move through families stems from his love for us. And clearly, in his love and wisdom, God ordains that the way parents choose to relate to God impacts children and grandchildren. When the Lord revealed himself to Moses, he said it again:

*The Lord, the Lord, a God merciful and gracious,
slow to anger, and abounding in steadfast love
and faithfulness, keeping steadfast love for
thousands, forgiving iniquity and transgression
and sin, but who will by no means clear the
guilty, visiting the iniquity of the fathers on the
children and the children's children, to the third
and the fourth generation* (Exodus 34:6-7).

At this point we may ask, does this mean God holds us accountable for the sins of our ancestors? In many places in the Bible God assures us he will not do this. In Deuteronomy, he decrees, "Fathers shall not be put to death because of their children, nor shall children be put to death because of their fathers" (24:16).

And in Ezekiel he explains, "Behold, all souls are mine; the soul of the father as well as the soul of the son is mine: the soul who sins shall die" (Ezekiel 18:2-4). He affirms the same thing again in Jeremiah, "everyone shall die for his own iniquity" (Jeremiah 31:30).

So, by allowing the broader teaching of the Bible to help us interpret these verses about family sin, we can conclude that while the sins of our ancestors affect us intensely, God holds each person solely accountable for his own sin.

How Does Family Sin Affect Us?

Molded to Fit

On a natural level, a parent's sinful choices create an influential environment. If we are like clay shaped as we grow, our family environment is our mold. Whatever we grew up in feels to us like a "fit."

This makes the search for a spouse a precarious journey.

Because when we meet a man or woman whose personality contours match the mold that shaped us, we often think we have fallen in love. But what we are actually experiencing is the chemistry of finding a "fit." Then we may drown in dismay as our marriage turns out nearly identical to the family that shaped us.

If our mother tried to please a series of abusers, her choices shaped us so a relationship with an abuser, though terrifying and painful, feels natural. We choose it, just like she did. If we were sexually or physically abused in our family home, remaining the victim or becoming the perpetrator of the same kind of abuse also feels, on an unconscious level, normal.

So, having been shaped by our family of origin, apart from the transforming work of God, we are inclined to perpetuate the sins and mistakes of our parents and grandparents.

The Wounds We Carry

We can come at this another way by considering the wounds we received in our families. Our parents' and grandparents' sin can wound us through abuse, neglect, hyper-criticism, perfectionism, enmeshment, or abandonment. Hurting, we are tempted to find sinful or self-destructive ways to seek relief for our pain. We also may live with a pernicious bent to recreate the conditions of our "failures" in order to "get it right" and gain a sense of mastery over what crushed us.

A boy whose dad is never home may turn to drugs to assuage the ache of rejection. Victims of abuse may attempt to mitigate a sense of shame and helplessness by abusing someone else. The pain of having never pleased his mother might drive a man into the arms of another critical woman where he continues striving to earn that elusive affirmation. Or a woman whose dad did not delight in her beauty may devote herself to cultivating her physical appearance and choose men who value only her looks—to the destruction of her heart.

Family Sin and the Demonic

Family sin can have another destructive effect. Demons given access to the family system can oppress one generation after another by intensifying temptations to certain kinds of sin or pounding on the minds and hearts of children with the same lies that wounded the parents or grandparents.

Demons can gain access to family systems through willful, repetitive sin and occult activities. When someone chooses—over and over—to indulge a sinful desire, it is as if they slowly wear away their God-given immune system to demonic oppression. As a result, demons associated with that sin may eventually attach themselves to that person to intensify his or her bondage.

A man who begins by enjoying pornography on the internet may find himself gripped by increasing lust drawing him to strip bars and then to prostitutes. A woman who cherishes bitterness toward her sister may grow in anger toward a list of people until her rage blows out in regular blasts over her children and family. Because demons have earned a foothold in these families, the children of this man and woman may also battle lust and anger.

Parents who experiment with occult practices like using a Ouija board, having their palms read, pronouncing curses (calling on forces of evil to cause harm to someone else), or reciting mantras, open a door in the spiritual world for demons to pass into their family systems.

These demons may perpetuate their oppression and temptation through the generations until someone in the family line confesses and repents of the sin, renounces the occult activity, or commands the demons to leave as I describe in the chapter on demonic oppression. With these prayers and commands we close the doors to the demonic and invite the life-giving power of the Holy Spirit into our families. I will give you examples of such prayers in the spiritual exercises following this chapter.

God's Life Breaks In

When the Lord grafts his life and love into a family tree, he releases us from family sin and demonic interference. Peter celebrates this reality, encouraging his young church, "you were ransomed from the futile ways inherited from your forefathers" (1 Peter 1:18).

God's Spirit wants to produce in us his fruit: "love, joy, peace, patience, kindness, goodness, faithfulness, gentleness, self-control" (Galatians 5:22-23). He longs to free us from everything unholy that might come down through our family: "sexual immorality, impurity, sensuality, idolatry, sorcery, enmity, strife, jealousy, fits of anger, rivalries, dissensions, divisions, envy, drunkenness, orgies, and things like these" (Galatians 5:19-21). He desires to cultivate through us a legacy like Paul celebrated in Timothy's family: "I long to see you, that I may be filled with joy. I am reminded of your sincere faith, a faith that dwelt first in your grandmother Lois and your mother Eunice and now, I am sure, dwells in you as well" (2 Timothy 1:4-5).

We can cooperate with God in producing such fruit in our hearts and in our families by growing in self-awareness, resistance to temptation, and vision for a different life for our children than we may have had. We can also practice prayers of confession, repentance, and renunciation. Together with God we can tear down stones of family sin and make clear pathways for legacies rich in God's beautiful character.

Drawing a Family Tree

Now I'd like you to skip ahead to the spiritual exercise for day one where I ask you to create a family tree.[30] Please use whatever format feels comfortable for you. You may have better computer skills than I do and find it simple to craft something digitally. You can also use blank paper or poster board.

Before you begin please ask the Holy Spirit to give you insight into patterns of grace and faith as well as patterns of sin or oppression in your family. Prayerfully consider each person you know about in your family—your immediate family, your spouse's family if you are married, your grandparents, aunts, uncles, and great-grandparents if you know anything about them.

Record near each person's name their legacy of family sin and family faith. You might remember Aunt Rhoda neglected her family, Grandma Smith was an alcoholic, and Uncle Jim gave away candy to street children. Maybe Grandma Smith also prayed for each family member by name every day she spent in the nursing home. I think you will be surprised what comes to mind. Feel free to inquire of other people in your family regarding things you may not be as familiar with as they are. Take as much time as you need for this project.

Please remember two things about the people you are thinking about. They are frail and human, just like you and me. And you are not harming them or doing anything wrong by naming the sins that characterized their lives. When you finish this exercise, you can destroy this family tree.

As you pray and think about your family, consider these possible patterns of family sin, occult involvement, or harmful relationships:

- Family Sin: anger at God, false religions, pride, materialism, judgmental attitudes, racism, bitterness, rage, hatred of men or women, unforgiveness, perfectionism, cold love, addiction

- Occult Activities: Ouija Boards, tarot cards, palm readings, séances, evil movies or music, Satan worship, levitation, casting spells, pronouncing curses

- Harmful relationships: divorce, suicide, abortion, estrangement, mockery, pregnancy out of wedlock, manipulation, control, abuse, murder, prostitution, promiscuity, pornography use, lust

You may be startled to see how some of these sins resurface throughout your family tree.

But please also pray and consider the ways the Lord may have woven patterns of grace and life through your family tree:

- Family Faith: Did anyone in your family tree love God, pray for your family, teach children and grandchildren truth from the Bible, or encourage church attendance? Did anyone exercise tremendous faith? Have great peace in trusting God? Or die a joyful death, anticipating the face of Jesus?

- Godly Character: Did anyone in your family give generously? Forgive easily? Love sacrificially? Was anyone full of joy? Did anyone make you feel loved and safe? Was anyone brave?

Take Heart

Much of what happens in our families we take for granted, excuse, or ignore. I hope by creating your family tree you have gained insight into possible stones of family sin or oppression obstructing your growth in God's joy and love. I know this can be distressing. So I want to encourage you that this can also be an exciting time for you. God may be giving you glimpses of a new vision for the path ahead, a path of freedom from family sins that until now you just accepted as the way things must be. If so, the tree your children's children draw may look very different from yours.

I also hope you find reasons for worship and gratitude as you survey your tree. Maybe you are the first in your family to experience life in God, and you recognize what he has rescued you from. Or perhaps you see how love, faith, and prayer have woven their way through the branches to reach you. In the prayers at the end of this chapter, you will have opportunity to thank God for these branches of life.

Confessing and Renouncing for Your Family

The Bible contains accounts of many people praying representational prayers. Moses, Nehemiah, Ezra, and Daniel, for example, confessed as their own the sins of Israel. The stories show the Lord honoring and answering such prayers.

Daniel prayed, "To us, O Lord, belongs open shame, to our kings, to our princes, and to our fathers, because *we* have sinned against you. To the Lord our God belong mercy and forgiveness, for *we* have rebelled against him and have not obeyed the voice of the Lord our God by walking in his laws" (Daniel 9:8-10, emphasis added). Daniel lived righteously in exile, but he confessed before the Lord the sins of his people as his own.

And Gabriel, God's angel, came to Daniel to tell him that his pleas for mercy had been heard by God: "O Daniel, I have now come out to give you insight and understanding. At the beginning of your pleas for mercy a word went out, and I have come to tell it to you, for you are greatly loved" (Daniel 9:22-23).

In the spiritual exercises at the end of this chapter, I give you outlines of prayers you can use to confess to God the family sin you identified as you created your family tree. Some of this sin you may know you share with your family. Some you may not. Even so, I encourage you to confess and renounce it like Moses and Daniel did. In ways I don't pretend to grasp, God sometimes honors such prayer by shattering patterns of demonic oppression in families. This is especially true when the sin involves false religions or occult practices. Praying in these ways may send away any demons afflicting you or family members.

Marcy's Story

Marcy came to our healing prayer team to seek help during a time of intense stress in her family. The team asked her to create a family tree, like I have asked you to do. She was skeptical about this practice, especially about confessing sin on behalf of her family, but as she completed her tree, she was startled to see patterns of family sin three generations deep. Longing for her children to experience freedom from these patterns, she went ahead with the prayers of confession in the presence of the team.

One of the patterns she noticed descended from her grandmother's family. Her grandmother grew up in Nazi Germany, and her grandmother's brothers had served in the Nazi youth movement. Marcy's grandmother had deep disdain for people and often spoke in hateful ways about people she saw as different from herself. Marcy saw this same tendency in parts of her extended family. So as part of her confession, she confessed disdain and prejudice.

When she said these words, Marcy suddenly felt nauseated and thought she might throw up. Her prayer minister, thinking these physical symptoms might indicate demonic interference, commanded any spirits of disdain or prejudice attached to Marcy to leave. Marcy felt a fluttering in her chest and then peace.

Immediately Marcy felt the eyes of her heart were opened to recognize the same patterns of disdain and prejudice in her immediate family. She saw her family shared a tendency to view themselves with elitism, pride, and self-righteousness while looking down on or feeling threatened by people they viewed as different.

But since that time, this pattern has changed, and Marcy describes with joy the way her children embrace and love "the outsider, the odd ball, the young person struggling to fit in, and the lost." She says, "When God removed this spirit of disdain and prejudice, he opened my eyes to the beauty of people in process and to the pursuing love of God that is not put off by dirt and grime." She now heartily encourages people to pray prayers of confession over family sin.

My Prayer for You

I pray as you move through the prayers at the end of this chapter God will fill you with the joy that must have filled Daniel's heart when he heard, "You are greatly loved." I pray any systems of family sin or oppression that have stood like stones between you and God's loving heart toward you may be torn down. And I pray, with the writer of Hebrews, you may have God's help to "lay aside every weight, and sin which clings so closely," and "run with endurance the race that is set before you, looking to Jesus, the founder and perfecter of your faith" (Hebrews 12:1-2). Amen.

Spiritual Exercises for Chapter Nine

Creating a Family Tree

1. Make Ephesians 3:14-20 a prayer for your family. Then ask the Lord to show you the patterns of sin and faith in your family. Ask him also to show you, as you create your family tree, that you are greatly loved.

2. Using whatever format you feel comfortable with—a poster board, blank paper, or your computer—draw a family tree. Include yourself, your children if you have any, your spouse or former spouses if you have been married, your parents, aunts and uncles, grandparents, and great-grandparents. For each person on the tree, prayerfully consider their legacy of sin and/or faith and record these things near their name. Please refer to the lists provided in the chapter to prompt your thinking. You may take as much time as you need for this activity.

3. Now sit back and look over the tree you have created. Ask the Lord to help you see what he sees in your family. You may want to use colored pencils to trace patterns of sin and faith as you see them emerge.

4. Tell the Lord how you feel about what you see. Ask him to assure you of his love and help you to know how to pray or what to do with what he has shown you.

Prayers of Thanksgiving, Confession, Renunciation, and Blessing

Note: You may pray these prayers alone. However, there is more power in praying together with someone. I encourage you to seek a mentor or faithful, praying friend to join you as you pray through these prayers.

A Prayer of Protection

I bring myself under the authority and protection of Jesus Christ my Lord. I surrender myself fully to him and declare my intention that he be lord over my body, my heart, my soul, and my life. I ask, Lord, that you protect me from the evil one "by the power of your name" (John 17:11 NIV). And in the powerful name of Jesus I command any demonic spirits determined to interfere with these prayers to leave me now. I command you to present yourselves to Jesus and to do whatever he tells you to do. By faith I bring myself under the shed blood of Jesus which cancels the power of evil and of sin. I ask you, Lord, to protect me and my family from any evil attack. I trust you to be my shield and my rock. Amen.

A Prayer of Thanksgiving

Father in heaven, "from whom every family in heaven and on earth is named" (Ephesians 3:15), I thank you for the people in my family, _____, who loved you, prayed for our family, taught us about you, and left a legacy of faith, hope, and love. I thank you for graciously breaking into my family to save me and lead me out of darkness into your marvelous light (1 Peter 2:9). I thank you for rescuing me from the sin and oppression in my family, and I thank you that you will rescue my children as well.

I pray that you would strengthen me and everyone in my family through your Spirit in our inner beings, so that Christ may dwell in our hearts through faith—that we, being rooted and grounded in love, may have strength to comprehend with all the saints what is the breadth and length and height and depth, and to know the love of Christ that surpasses knowledge, that we may be filled with all the fullness of God. Now to you who are able to do far more abundantly than all that we ask or think, according to the power at work within us, to you be glory in the church, and in my family, and in Christ Jesus throughout all generations, forever and ever. Amen. (From Ephesians 3:14-21)

Confession

I confess to you, Holy Father, the patterns of family sin and harmful relationships you have shown me. I confess that I or members of my family have made a practice of the sins of _____
_____ *(name the family sins you identified)*. I also confess that I or members of my family have not loved others as you have commanded because we have engaged in harmful relational patterns such as _____ *(name the harmful relational patterns)*. I repent of these sins in my family line, and I renounce them. Please be the Lord of me and my family. Please forgive us and free us from these sins and relational patterns. I declare my desire that my family turn from these sins and harmful patterns and live to please you. I ask, Father, for you to fill me and my family with the power of your Holy Spirit so that we may find victory in these areas where we have experienced defeat. In the name and power of Jesus Christ I pray. Amen.

Confessing Occult Activities

Holy Father, I confess the sins of occult involvement in my family. I, or members of my family, have acted in unbelief and disobedience, seeking spiritual power from sources other than you by _____
_____ *(name the occult practices or false religions in your family*

tree). Lord, please forgive us for these occult practices. I acknowledge before you the evil I or members of my family have committed and I renounce all occult involvement. I ask you, Lord, in mercy, to forgive us these offenses against you. Help me, Lord, and each person in my family, to avoid any such practice in the future. Please free us from any demonic attachment we invited through these practices and protect us from evil by the power of your name. In the name of Jesus Christ I nullify any invitation any member of my family made to the demonic and I cancel the assignment of any occult demon sent against me or my family. I declare that the God and Father of my Lord Jesus is the one, true, and living God, and I bring my family under his authority, that he would be our only Lord and our protector from this day forward. Please, Lord, may your kingdom come and your will be done in my family, that from this day forward your kingdom may be advanced through us. Amen.

A Prayer for Children in Your Family

I pray now for the children_____
(*name them*) in my family. I place these precious young ones in your loving hands, Father, and I pray that you would use the power of the cross to rescue them from any plans the evil one has against them. Please place over them the blood of your son and may his cross stand forever between them and your enemies. I pray that through them you would spread everywhere the fragrance of the knowledge of Christ. May all of your good purposes for their lives be fulfilled and may they, being delivered from the hand of their enemies, serve you without fear, in holiness and righteousness before you all of their days

(Luke 1:74-75). In the name of Jesus Christ. Amen.

A Final Prayer of Thanksgiving

I thank you, Father in heaven, for hearing my prayers today. I thank you for your redeeming love at work in my family. Thank you that I can trust you to heal my family of these sins and deliver us from our enemies. May your kingdom come and your will be done in my family as it is in heaven, and I rejoice in your authority and protection. Amen.

Discussion Questions for Chapter Nine:
The Stone of Family Sin

1. Have you been perplexed to see patterns of family sin passing down through the generations of families you know?

2. Have you seen God's power break into a family tree and bring positive changes?

3. How does it strike you that while we are only responsible for our own sin, we may be impacted by the sins of those in the generations preceding us?

4. Talk about your experience creating a family tree.

5. Can you see the movement of God in the generations of your family?

6. Do you see areas of sin or oppression being passed down in your family?

7. Did you pray through the prayers at the end of this chapter? Please share your experience.

Chapter Ten
The Stone of Unhealed Memories

"The Lord is my shepherd...He restores my soul."
~ Psalm 23:1, 3

The Power of Unhealed Memories

Well-meaning people sometimes say, "Time heals all wounds." But they do not speak the truth. Time alone heals nothing. Damaging experiences sink into our memories, possibly out of consciousness, but they live on with the power to poison our attitude toward ourselves and others and block God's love from warming our hearts. The power of these painful memories endures until Jesus touches and heals them.

I understand you may feel dismay as you begin this chapter, thinking I will ask you to revisit events you would rather not bring to mind. But until the tenderness of Jesus reaches you in these dark places, they may continue to shape your life in destructive ways. I long for his truth, his light, and his healing touch to roll away any stones of unhealed memories limiting your capacity for the love of God. I pray you will be able to press forward with courage and hope.

The way our bodies heal from physical injuries can help us understand the endurance of emotional wounds. Imagine you go camping in the mountains. The air turns chilly, so you grab the ax to chop kindling for a fire. You swing for the log but miss and sink the blade deep into your leg. Peeling away your torn pants, you see a laceration six inches long. A bit of your shin bone shows and blood soaks your socks and shoes.

You need someone to cleanse your wound and stitch it closed to keep germs out. Though you resent the inconvenience of the trip to the hospital, you go, knowing your leg will heal, the pain of the injury fading as the wound closes over. Soon after, you resume the activities that give you and others joy, like camping. Months later, when your little boy accidentally whacks you in the same spot with his toy baseball bat, you feel only the sting of the plastic bat, and you fake hopping around in pain just to tease him.

Now imagine that in this same situation, you don't seek medical treatment for your gash and instead wrap it in an old t-shirt and finish your camping trip. What happens?

The wound turns red, bacteria festers into an infection, and your pain intensifies. Weeks later, a layer of skin seals the wound and stops the bleeding, but you limp and struggle with fatigue and reduced immune function because your body loses energy fighting the constant infection. When your family wants to go camping again, you decline because of your pain and you may take offense at their "insensitivity." Your wound now defines your life.

Beyond that, what happens when that baseball bat smacks it a few months later? You will experience agony because of the compounded pain from the bat, *plus* the ax wound *plus* the infection. You may involuntarily scream at your son for his carelessness. You will have more pain in that moment than you felt on the camping trip, and your son will stand blinking in confusion and dismay.

Unhealed memories work similarly. We all receive emotional wounds. We may wield the ax ourselves, or someone else may swing it, or it may fly due to the accidental, tragic events of life in a fallen world. Regardless, experiences of abandonment, abuse, cruel words, humiliation, fear, loss, or shame wound us all. When this happens, if we or the people around us know how to "clean the wound" and "stitch it up" so it heals properly, we can recover with remarkable resiliency. In the case of emotional wounding, this involves bringing the event into the light where it can be talked about with a trusted person; receiving forgiveness if the event involves our sin; extending forgiveness if someone has sinned against us; and receiving prayer so that the Spirit of God can minister to our fear, rejection, or shame.

Most of us, however, do not receive help for our emotional wounds; life rolls on, and our painful experiences fester like the neglected ax wound. The memory of the painful event may sink out of our conscious memory, but its trauma remains in our heart like a pus-filled abscess—leaking poisonous emotions, empowering lies, and possibly providing footholds for demons to gain influence over us. We twist our ways of living, akin to limping or avoiding activities that cause us distress. And as we go along, when someone or something "bumps" that old spot, we react out of our excruciating pain.

An unhealed memory blocks our heart from God's heart by creating a reality for us that is not God's reality. Our heart hurts, living the pain of the infected wound—the heart's reality. God's love may brush the surface but not reach the needy area because the layer of skin over the wound keeps it out. Healing of memories is akin to a surgery where we open the wound and allow him to clean it and stitch it so it can heal. As he does this, he destroys the power of that memory to poison us and block God's love from reaching us. The stone of the unhealed memory rolls away, and we soak up his love and live in his reality.

How Do We Know If We Have Unhealed Memories?

Our emotional life gives us clues if we have memories in

need of healing: we may have great anxiety about things that do not cause others fear; we may rage about things our spouse considers inconsequential; we may be shamed by the slightest criticism; we may be compulsive about work or cleanliness; and we may never be able to receive God's love, no matter how often we hear about it. Our lifestyle and reactions seem natural to us, given our pain. But those around us, if they are honest, will say the degree of emotion we display in certain situations confuses them, or they may point out mysterious compensations in the way we live. Any of these clues may indicate we have unhealed memories standing as stones between God's heart and ours.

Humility and Faith

We'd like to think we would all quickly line up for this kind of heart surgery from God, but not necessarily. Bringing our painful memories to the Lord requires humility and faith.

We face a strong temptation when we feel pain to look to our immediate surroundings for the culprit, to blame *that* person or *that* circumstance. It must be YOU, we say, to our emotionally checked-out spouse, rebellious teenager, overbearing boss, disappointing pastor, or unpleasant circumstances. But this is analogous to blaming the boy with the bat for the pain of the infected ax wound.

Humility allows us to consider whether our unhealed issues make someone "bumping against" us more painful than necessary. If we have this humility, we can stop blaming for a moment and ask the Lord if our distress is disproportionate. Did our husband arriving fifteen minutes late for dinner warrant the silent treatment we gave him for the next two hours? Or did his tardiness hurt so much because someone in our past did not keep promises? If we realize our reactions are disproportionate, the Lord has provided a clue that he wants to heal something in our hearts.

Faith woos us into the tender presence of God where we can let down our defenses and allow our most painful, shameful, fearful memories to come to the surface. We have worked hard to keep these memories down. Allowing them to surface takes faith in the gentleness and compassion of Jesus.

I pray the Lord will give you both humility and faith so you can open your heart to him and let him roll away the stones of your unhealed memories with his healing love.

The Healing Presence of Jesus

Memories are stored in the realm of the heart, so they do not respond to reason. As Blaise Pascal observed, "The heart has its reasons which reason does not know." We cannot say to our heart, "Well, now you are grown-up and you know these things happen to lots of people. God loves you and you are fine." The heart does not hear you. It lives from its memories—replete with emotion and symbolism. When we seek God for healing of our painful memories, we give him access to our heart's stores of symbolic meaning and feeling.

In prayer, we can go back to a memory of shame or fear and invite Jesus to reveal himself to us there. His presence in a painful memory heals it. The power of that memory to haunt, poison, or influence us drains away.

Charles Kraft explains:

> Though Jesus was there when a wounding event took place, we probably felt alone, dependent entirely on our own resources. We neither saw him nor felt his presence at that time. During ministry, however, Jesus graciously enables us to feel his presence and, usually, to see him in the event. Though he doesn't change the event itself, the awareness of his presence is usually

sufficient to bring healing to even the most damaged memory.[31]

Sean and Lily

Sean remembers bringing his middle school report card home to his father. Sean was happy his report card had six As and one B+ on it. But his father glanced at it, flipped it aside, and demanded, "What happened?" Sean's heart flooded with rage and shame. He vowed his father would never say that to him again, and he went through high school, college, and graduate school with nearly perfect grades. He was often sick or suffering from ulcers, driven by a terror of "failure."

In prayer Sean asked the Lord into that memory. Immediately, Sean saw Jesus sitting in the chair where his father had been. With trepidation, he handed Jesus the report card. Jesus also tossed the report card aside, but he opened his arms to Sean and said with a big smile, "I *missed* you while you were at school today!" Sean ran into Jesus's arms and received the love his father had been unable to show him. Healing this memory, the Lord healed part of Sean's need to be perfect to feel worthy of love.

Lily experienced a healing like this in the parking lot near a softball field. Lily's baby died when he was nine months old, and ten years later Lily remained troubled. One of our prayer ministers ran into Lily before a game, and she shared with him about her seemingly endless pain. He was in the process of telling her how Jesus helps people with their painful memories when Lily saw herself in the hospital room, holding her baby as he died, her heart agonized by grief and pain. And she saw Jesus standing behind her with his hands outstretched. She wept tears of joy and looked up at my friend. "It's okay," she exclaimed, "I see him! He was there. He was there!" Joy flooded her heart along with the certainty that her son lives with Jesus in heaven. She ran to tell her family about it. A year later, she remains so touched by the healing Jesus gave her she can't talk about it without weeping. Jesus drained away the crippling grief of that memory and replaced it with comfort and joy.

Over and over we see Jesus do this. He may shine light into a dark memory, speak a healing word, or give a frightened or wounded person a hug. When he does these things, the memory no longer has the same power. It is as if, in our hearts from that day forward, Jesus was there to clean the wound and stitch it up so no infection could fester in it.

Additional Dimensions of Healing of Memories

Many times Jesus heals painful memories simply by appearing in them, as he did for Sean and Lily. But we have found four other avenues of prayer to explore if a memory remains painful:

- **Forgiveness**
  Sometimes the power of unhealed memories comes from the failure to receive forgiveness (please see the chapter on guilt) or the failure to extend forgiveness (please see the chapter on forgiveness).

- **Lies**
  We must ask the Lord to reveal any lies we believed at the time of this wounding and ask him to replace them with his truth (please refer to the chapter regarding lies).

- **Vows**
  When we experience trauma we sometimes make a vow in response. We might say, "I will never let anyone get close

enough to hurt me again," or "I will never forgive her," or "I will get perfect grades." When we live by a vow like this, the vow becomes our ruling principle and prevents us from trusting God. But we can break the power of such vows by confessing them to the Lord and renouncing them.

- **Demonic Attachment**
  Demons can use the buried lies, vows, unforgiveness, and pain associated with an unhealed memory as footholds for oppression. But when Jesus brings healing, forgiveness, and truth and helps us break the vows, the demons have nothing left to use. We can command them to leave. (Please see the chapter on demonic oppression.)

Some memories need healing in all these dimensions, others in just one, but it is helpful to be aware of these different elements.

The Mystery of Memory

Our memories function mysteriously. A survival mechanism in our psyches allows us to bury overpowering experiences in our subconscious so we can function without them haunting our daily lives. In this case, we have no recall of the traumatic event. But just because we cannot remember what happened does not mean the trauma ceases to influence us. For this reason, the Holy Spirit sometimes brings to mind a long forgotten scene from our childhood because he knows its power and wants to heal it.

We also may experience a mystery of memory called disassociation. In this case, we remember the event, but we bury the powerful emotions we experienced when it happened. If we have done this, we may be fooled into thinking that we are "over" that event. This was the case with me for a long time.

You know about my head injury. For most of my life I could describe to you how I fell, pieces of my skull lodged in my brain, I nearly died, and I wore a helmet for nine years—in the manner I would use if I read you a clipping from the classified ads. But, in a time of prayer, the Lord connected the events of the accident with my buried feelings, and I shocked myself as I wept through torrents of grief, sorrow, and fear. Recently, I had to ask my husband not to invite me to tell the story of my accident when we are getting to know new people. I do not find it so easy to rattle off an account of that traumatic time.

False Memories

Our memories function a little like our dreams in that they don't emanate from our rational selves, but from the parts of us that function symbolically. Like an artist, they may generate exaggerated or shocking images to make a point.

When I was in a controlling and emotionally dangerous romantic relationship, I had recurring dreams about rats. I kept seeing them crawling on my body. My heart—repulsed by the unhealthy relationship—expressed its distress through this imagery. When we feel out of control we may dream about airplanes crashing. We may dream about being naked in public places when we feel vulnerable. As my children started middle school I had nightmares about them being lost in big, dangerous cities.

Sometimes our memory functions the same way. If we understand this, it can be helpful; if we misunderstand, we can get into trouble.

The symbolic function of memory helps us when one memory serves as a symbol for a collection of memories. When the Lord heals the one memory, all the memories connected to it heal as well. If your father was emotionally unavailable, you may have a memory surface—a picture of your dad with the newspaper in front of his face. Through prayer, the Lord may help you forgive him for reading the newspaper when you needed his attention; Jesus may help you receive forgiveness for hating your father or rebelling against him because of his inattention; the Lord may also appear to you in that memory, showing you his love and removing the feelings of worthlessness that took root as your father ignored you. Then—because that one memory represents a childhood of similar memories—all of the wounds you received from your father's emotional unavailability may be healed along with it! The Lord doesn't need to call up and heal years of memories one at a time.

But the symbolic function of memory can get us into trouble when our heart produces a "memory" that is not actually a memory, but is symbolic—like dreams. I had this happen to me.

As a prayer minister prayed with me, a picture of me at age four flashed into my mind. I stood in my preschool playroom with blood pouring out of a wound on my head and streaming over my face. My mouth was open wide in a silent scream of terror. I stopped praying and my eyes flew open. I told the prayer minister what I saw and asked, "Do you think something happened to me at preschool?" (Remember I had buried my emotions about my accident.)

The prayer minister had the wisdom to ask, "How old were you at the time of your accident?"

"Oh," I whispered, "I was four." I fell in May of my preschool year.

In astonishment I understood my heart had generated this picture of how I felt when I got hurt. This was not a *factual* memory. I did not get hurt at school and my head did not bleed. But this "memory" was *true* in that it symbolized how my heart responded when I got hurt.

Knowing memories can function this way, we must be discerning and not leap to conclusions about surprising images or "memories" our hearts produce.

The Biblical Basis for Healing of Memories

Jesus says loving God with all of our heart, soul, mind, and strength and loving our neighbor as ourselves are the two most important commandments (Matthew 22:37-38). And John says, "We love because he first loved us" (1 John 4:19).

Our unhealed memories can make it difficult for us to obey these commandments. We may be like an adopted child with an attachment disorder. No matter how much love our new family (God and his people) showers upon us, it cannot penetrate because our wounds make us suspicious and guarded against giving and receiving love. Since God knows our unhealed memories block his love from getting to us, he makes a way to heal them so we can drop our guard, receive his love, and obey his most important commandments.

The biblical writers testify to this sort of healing. David says, "He restores my soul," in Psalm 23. He crafts a beautiful picture in this psalm: with his heart (soul) restored from damage and wounds, he can delight in the loving care of the good shepherd.

When Jesus began his public ministry he used this passage from Isaiah to describe his purpose:

> *The Spirit of the Lord God is upon me, because the Lord has anointed me to bring good news to the poor; he has sent me to bind up the brokenhearted, to proclaim liberty to the captives, and the opening of the prison to those who are bound. . . to comfort all who mourn; to grant to those who mourn in Zion—to give them a beautiful headdress instead of ashes, the oil of gladness instead of mourning, the garment of praise instead of a faint spirit; that they may be called oaks of righteousness, the planting of the Lord, that he may be glorified* (Isaiah 61:1-3).

These verses graciously testify to the healing and freeing work of Jesus through the Holy Spirit. He heals broken hearts, comforts the grieving, and frees the bound. His restored people overflow with praise and gladness and give glory to the Lord. Healing our most painful memories is part of this process.

Peter's story shows Jesus doing this for one man. We talked about Peter's story earlier, exploring how his mask shattered the night he denied Jesus. I return to this chapter in Peter's life here to emphasize that to restore Peter, Jesus heals his friend's searing memories of denial and shame. Remember, Peter fails spectacularly the night before Jesus's crucifixion. While he warms himself at a charcoal fire, people standing around ask him three times if he is with Jesus. Each time he denies it. When he realizes what he has done, he goes outside, weeping desperately (Matthew 26:75). This shameful memory could have crippled Peter's ability to lead Jesus's Church.

But after the resurrection, Jesus finds Peter fishing, builds a charcoal fire, sits Peter near it, and asks him—three times—"do you love me?" Each time, Peter affirms his love for Jesus, the last time crying out, "Lord, you know everything; you know that I love you." And each time, Jesus affirms his trust in Peter, saying, "Feed my lambs. Tend my sheep. Feed my sheep" (John 21:15-17).

Jesus healed Peter's shameful memory of failure by recreating the scene and burning over the old one with a new memory: Peter experiences love, forgiveness, and commissioning—at a charcoal fire. And Jesus gives Peter the opportunity to wash away his shameful denials by telling his lord—three times—how Peter loves him. By healing Peter's most painful memory, Jesus empowered him to lead the first church in Jerusalem.

A Final Encouragement

Returning to our story of the wounded leg, imagine we finally got treatment and the leg has healed. But we had that wound for a long time, so we learned crooked ways of walking. The muscles in our legs and back need to relearn correct posture. In fact, limping might feel easier. But we no longer have to limp. We have a choice. Will we stand up straight and walk?

Healing of memories often operates like this. When Jesus heals the memory, it doesn't mean we will never again feel tempted by old patterns and emotions. It means we see options, whereas prior to the healing we did not. Before our healing, we responded to threatening situations with anger or shame and saw no alternative. After, we will see another path—one created by the Spirit of God. We can choose patience and respond kindly. We can choose not to indulge the addiction. We can choose not to allow someone's careless remark to knock us into a pit of self-hatred or shame. But, *we still have to choose.*

We have to make new choices, retraining our emotional "muscles" to stand up straight and walk. We have to do the emotional equivalent of dancing with our spouse or playing baseball with our son, even if it at first it leaves us gasping for breath because we have avoided activity for so long. This is how, by faith, we walk into the new life of giving and receiving love the Lord healed us for.

May the Lord bless you as you explore whether stones of unhealed memories stand in the wall between God's heart and yours. May he free you from what lies behind so you may press on toward that for which Christ Jesus took hold of you, the upward call of God (Philippians 3:12-14).

Spiritual Exercises for Chapter Ten

Note: Sometimes the Lord heals memories as we seek him through solitary prayer, and these spiritual exercises are meant to facilitate such prayer. However, the process is more powerful when we pray with someone. If you sense you have deep, painful memories, I encourage you to seek the opportunity to pray with someone you trust or a team of people trained in inner healing prayer. You will be greatly helped by the loving presence of others as you recall the pain of your past.

What Would the Lord Like to Heal?

1. Make Psalm 23 your prayer. Let it help you remember and find comfort in the Lord's attentive and faithful care for you, even through valleys of the shadow of death (Psalm 23:4).

2. Is there someone you feel tempted to blame for your painful emotions? Which emotions does this person trigger in you: anger, shame, loneliness, self-hatred, the temptation to an addiction, the need to control, resentment? Or is there a situation that causes you inordinate anxiety, worry, fear, anger, or rage?

3. Pray something like this: "Lord, you can see these painful emotions of _____ that rise up in me. I know they are hindering my freedom to love you and my neighbor. I bring them to you. I am willing to allow that _____ (*a person*) or ___ _____ (*a situation*) is not entirely to blame for these feelings I have. I release _____ (*this person/this situation*) into your hands for now. My heart is open to whatever you want to show me about me."

4. Now ask the Lord to show you when you first experienced

these same painful emotions. Sit quietly with him, allowing him to surface a memory. Don't dismiss any scenes that come to mind. Sometimes the Lord will call up a seemingly benign or irrelevant memory to heal because he is gentle and does not want to overwhelm you.

5. If nothing comes to mind, that is okay. The Lord knows the perfect times and places for these things. You may pray something like this: "Lord, I trust myself to you. In your time and in your way, please guide me into all truth and free me to love and be loved. I give you permission to continue searching my heart and to show me whatever you know I need to see. Please make me attentive to your leading." You can also make Psalm 43:3-5 your prayer for as long as need be: "Send out your light and your truth; let them lead me; let them bring me to your holy hill and to your dwelling! Then I will go to the altar of God, to God my exceeding joy, and I will praise you with the lyre, O God, my God. Why are you cast down, O my soul, and why are you in turmoil within me? Hope in God; for I shall again praise him, my salvation and my God." Pay attention over the next days and weeks to anything the Lord brings to your mind. You might find yourself remembering something while you drive your car or cook dinner. If this happens, store that memory away to take to him in prayer when you have time.

Healing a Painful Memory

1. If the Lord has brought to your mind a memory and you want him to heal it, prepare your heart by prayerfully reading Isaiah 53:4-5. Take a few moments to thank the Lord for his willingness to share your suffering.

2. Now, in the presence of the Lord, allow the memory to come back to you. Put yourself in the memory and allow

the emotions you felt at the time to come to the surface.

3. Tell the Lord how you feel. Share with him your grief, sorrow, fear, hatred, or anything else that your heart experiences in remembering what happened to you.

4. Please ask the Lord to come into the memory with you. Wait for him. Watch and listen for what he will do or say.

5. When the time seems right, ask the Lord these questions:

   a. Is there someone I need to forgive in this memory?

   b. Do I need to confess anything to you and receive forgiveness for anything related to this memory?

   c. Did I believe any lies as a result of this memory?

   d. Please replace these lies with your truth. (Wait for him to speak or reveal truth to you.)

   e. Did I make a vow because of this memory? (If so, renounce them, saying, "In the name of Jesus, I renounce the vow I made to _____. I break this vow and I trust myself to the Lord alone to provide for me and protect me. Lord, teach me to walk in obedience to you and to no longer live by this vow.")

   f. Has this memory provided a foothold for any demonic attachment? If so, command the demonic spirit to leave in the name of Jesus Christ. (See the chapter on demonic oppression if you need help.)

   g. Is there anything else you want to show me, Lord?

6. Thank the Lord for what he has done for you. Ask him to fill you with his Holy Spirit, to seal what he has done in your heart, and to help you learn new ways of living now that this memory has been healed.

Discussion Questions for Chapter Ten:
The Stone of Unhealed Memories

1. What have you been taught about "time heals all wounds"?

2. Have you ever recognized you are "bumping" someone else's old wounds or they are "bumping" yours?

3. Do you think you ever emotionally overreact? Please explain.

4. Have you ever had a dream reveal to you the way your heart feels? Please explain.

5. Did you have long forgotten memories arise as you read this chapter?

6. What stood out to you in Peter's story about healing of memories?

7. Do you have experience with using new emotional "muscles" as the Lord helped you to change an area of your life?

Chapter Eleven
The Stone of Anger at God

"My God, my God, why have you forsaken me?
Why are you so far from saving me,
from the words of my groaning?"
~ Psalm 22:1

"The reason the mass of men fear God,
and at bottom dislike *Him,*
is because they rather distrust His heart
and fancy Him all brain like a watch."
~ Herman Melville

Now we will look at the largest stone in the wall between my heart and God's heart, a stone found in the hearts of masses of Christians and non-Christians alike—the stone of anger at God.

We read and hear about God's goodness and love. Yet we get sick. We lose our jobs. People we love die. Children in our cities take guns to school and kill their classmates and teachers. And Muslim extremists spread terror. Facing the evils of random brutality and inevitable death, our hearts revolt: either there is no God, or he does not care.

How many times have you heard someone say, "I refuse to believe in a God who would allow...the holocaust/sexual abuse/ the Rwandan genocide/my dad to die..."? I suspect anger at God over evil and suffering fuels, at some level, the thought-process of every modern person who rejects God. And, as my story will show, this anger can remain firmly planted in the heart of a Christian as well.

The problem is Christians sometimes hide this stone. Unlike those who openly reject God, we revere him. We can be reluctant to admit, even to ourselves, if we are angry at him. We might push our anger down and away, never acknowledging we are angry at him; we may not even know we are. But we cannot get close to him. Our anger—a large, unacknowledged stone—divides our heart from God's.

Before God helped me identify and tear down the stone of anger, I did not think I was angry with him. I just could not believe he loved me, and I lived in almost constant fear of bad things happening to me or those I loved.

My Aunt Nora and My Cousin Lauren

I've already talked a bit about my aunt and cousin. When I was thirteen my aunt Nora and my cousin Lauren fled the abuse of my uncle John and came to live with my family in Washington State for several months. Nora had a vivacious spirit. She rocked our old piano with ragtime music and filled our house with laughter.

My mom (her older sister) and my dad spent those months strengthening Nora's resolve to leave her destructive marriage. Nora returned to California determined to restart her life independent of John. Less than a week later, I got off the school bus on a warm spring afternoon, walked across the greening grass, and opened the door to our living room. I found my nine-year-old sister Heather huddled in a chair in front of the television. She looked at me with wide, frightened eyes.

"John killed Nora and Lauren," she said.

I sat down in the other chair and stared in silence at the television while the canned laughter of a sitcom rolled in waves over us.

My mom had already flown to California to keep vigil with her family as they waited in fear, hoping the police would catch John. She returned a week or so later, with no news of my uncle, but she brought a stack of newspaper articles about the murders. I had never heard the word "bludgeoned" before, but I read it over and over in the articles describing how he had beaten them to death. I also learned he had written profanities on the walls of his home with their blood.

My family reeled in shock and grief. A few weeks later, we got in our boat and travelled north to Alaska for another summer of salmon fishing. Then one evening the VHS radio crackled and a coast guard officer informed us we had a call from a landline in California. I heard my grandma's voice, small and thin, speaking to my mom. "They found John."

"What?" my mom asked.

The radio crackled, and her voice said again, "They found John."

My mom couldn't take it in.

"Mom, they found John," I said loudly.

I saw her lean on the dash for support. My grandma told her investigators found John's decomposing body in his car at the bottom of a cliff. Apparently he had raced over the edge not long after the murders.

Twenty–Five Years Later

I was thirty-eight years old, living in Colorado with my husband, Doug—a pastor—and our three children. I had lived as a committed Christian since I was eighteen. But on a date one night, I admitted to Doug I had no confidence God would take me to heaven. "I am afraid," I said, "when I face him at the end, he will throw me out."

"You. Are. Kidding. Me," he responded.

"No, I am not!" I confessed with pain in my heart.

And, as I have said, I had many other fears as well. I did not feel safe from any imaginable tragedy. Why in the world would I think it wouldn't happen to me?

I did not think of fear as unreasonable. After all, God never promises to protect us from all harm. But not long after this conversation with my husband, I thought I heard the Spirit of God whispering to me, "What would it be like to live without one single fear?" I felt as if he led me up to the top of my dark tower of fear to look on a world of sunshine and beauty and said, "Wouldn't you rather live out there?"

I did. I wanted to be free of fear, and I grew in the conviction that my fear was not right because the Lord promises me his protection and love. I began to ask him to tear down my stronghold of fear and let me know his love.

One evening a few weeks later I lay in bed almost asleep when a particularly painful bout of fear gripped me. I began to pray quietly, commanding the enemy to leave me alone. Doug heard me and said, "Let's pray right now."

We sat up and he prayed, commanding any spirit of fear attached to me to leave. All of a sudden I began to sob, mourning the murders of my aunt and cousin. A spirit of fear must have acted like a cork in a bottle, damming up my grief. The spirit left, and my grief flowed out. I cried for a long time.

Then Doug startled me by quietly asking if I needed to forgive God. My mind rebelled because I had never been aware of being angry at God, and I certainly did not think anyone could "forgive" God. But my heart stepped forward, and I realized in a flash I felt *deeply* angry at God. He had not protected my aunt, a Christian, or her daughter, from a brutal and gruesome death. Though I had never acknowledged it, even to myself, I held this against him.

I wept harder. My true heart and God finally met. I confessed to him my anger at him. I sensed Jesus showing me a picture of my aunt and cousin in heaven with him—healthy, whole, and happy. I felt him saying to me, "See? They are well. They would not change a thing because of their joy."

And then Jesus asked me, "Are we okay, you and me?"

I weep even writing this because I still cannot fathom the respect and tenderness of him asking me that question: "Are we okay?"

Jesus asks *me?* Jesus, with profound respect for my fear and pain, wants to know if *I* will make peace with *him?* I can only think of the words of David who cried out, "Such knowledge is too wonderful for me; it is high; I cannot attain it" (Psalm 139:6).

I want to be clear. He did not apologize to me. He simply wanted to know if, in light of Nora and Lauren's joy in heaven and the fact *they* do not regret their early deaths, I would lay down my anger toward him? Would I trust him?

"Yes," I wept. "Yes, forgive me for my anger at you. I give it up. We are okay."

Since the prayer time had taken such an unexpected turn, I did not believe we had finished praying to free me from fear. But I felt depleted and tired, and thinking we would pray more in the days to come, I lay down to sleep.

The Lord had something else in mind.

Moments later, a powerful awareness of his presence in my room startled me completely awake. I felt him standing near my bed, and in astonishment I sensed his exuberant delight. Somehow he poured his love into me—a joyous, cleansing, jubilant love—that filled me with gladness and drove out every single fear. I wept and laughed all at once. Heart-to-heart with Jesus I discovered he loves me—ardently. In wonder, gratitude, and humility, I marveled to discover Jesus desires me near him, longs for me, rejoices over me, and treasures me.

He took me in my memory to the house where Nora and Lauren died, and he met me there, freeing me from invisible chains that held me and embracing me. Then he carried me away and painted pictures in my mind of him and me together in a mountain meadow, dancing, celebrating, and sitting close. He streamed verses about his love into my mind: "I have loved you with an everlasting love" (Jeremiah 31:3) and "Arise, my love, my beautiful one, and come away" (Song of Songs 2:10).

Doug, trying to sleep next to me, became concerned because I was shaking with laughter and tears. "Are you okay?"

"The Lord won't let me sleep," I laughed with joy. "He's too excited."

I understood in that moment that my anger at God, an anger I had not even admitted I harbored, had kept him at arm's length most of my life. He did not let me sleep because of his joy. The wall had finally come down and his love could reach me. I sensed he didn't want to wait another minute.

The next morning I sat with the Lord and experienced again his delight in me as his Spirit directed me to scripture after scripture affirming his love for me. I felt reborn. Later my kids saw my delighted face. "Mommy's in love with Jesus," my daughter sang from her perch on the swing. Though I had been a Christian for thirty-two years, I felt so changed that it seemed, as I explained in chapter one, I had never understood the Christian life until that day.

At the root of all my fears was my fear God did not love me. A spirit of fear used the trauma of my accident, compounded by my aunt's murder, to lie to me about God's loving nature and convince me I was unlovable. When I couldn't trust God's love for me, everything was terrifying.

Five stones came down that night: the stone of my mask, a stone of demonic oppression, a stone of lies, a stone of anger at God, and a stone of unhealed memories. The stones came down. His love reached my heart. And fear went away, just as he promises: "Perfect love casts out fear" (1 John 4:18).

My new perspective did not mean I believed bad things would never happen to me. It just meant I knew—finally—he loved me. Knowing this, I had courage to face whatever might come. I didn't feel afraid.

I experienced this healing seven years ago. Since then, I have not lived in a rapturous state. I live what feels like a pretty normal life, with ups and downs, worries and troubles, like most everyone else I know. But since that day I do not doubt God loves me. Sometimes I have to work a little to remind myself, but I can *remember* he loves me. I can trust I belong to him and he will not throw me out when we meet at the end of my life on earth. I can trust he saves me from my sin through the sacrifice of his Son because he loves me. I treasure this wondrous gift of healing and do not take for granted that I can know God's love. I wrote this book because I want you to know it too.

The Constructive Power of Honesty

The Bible holds the prayers and cries of many who were angry and perplexed with God. Their honesty might shock modern readers:

- "My God, my God, why have you forsaken me?" (Psalm 22:1).

- "O Lord, God of my salvation; I cry out day and night before you…. You have put me in the depths of the pit, in the regions dark and deep. Your wrath lies heavy upon me, and you overwhelm me with all your waves…. Why do you cast my soul away? Why do you hide your face from me?" (Psalm 88:1, 6-7, 14).

- "O Lord, you have deceived me, and I was deceived" (Jeremiah 20:7).

- "I did not sit in the company of revelers, nor did I rejoice; I sat alone, because your hand was upon me, for you had filled me with indignation. Why is my pain unceasing, my wound incurable, refusing to be healed? Will you be to me like a deceitful brook, like waters that fail?" (Jeremiah 15:17-18).

These biblical writers poured out to God their questions, fear, anguish, and rage. They did not "curse God" as Job's wife commanded Job to do (Job 2:9), but they were authentic and transparent. They valued their relationship with God enough to be honest with him.

I don't like conflict. When I was a young woman, I couldn't have a conflictual conversation with anyone. I avoided hard topics, or I hid my face in my hands and cried during tough conversations I couldn't escape. But slowly I learned I did damage to my relationships when I had hard feelings toward someone and chose not to have a difficult conversation with them. By avoiding conflict, I took control of the relationship and chose to allow distance to grow between us. Contrary to my instincts, when we respectfully enter into an uncomfortable conversation, we choose the path toward sustaining and even growing the intimacy of any relationship.

The same is true in our relationship with God. If we deny our anger at him, or fail to talk to him about it, we put stones between his heart and ours. We *choose* a superficial relationship with him. To pursue closeness with him, we must bring him our anger and ask him our hard questions and wait for him to respond. In this way, we demonstrate we value our intimacy with him and trust him to care, listen, and respond.

A friend of mine did this when her fourteen-year-old son accidentally hanged himself in her basement. She raged at God one afternoon while she cleaned out her son's closet. "How could you take my son?" she cried.

She heard God say, "Would you rather I had never given him to you?"

My friend's grief changed at that point. She did not get the answer she wanted, but God's response altered her perspective. She saw the fourteen years she did get with her son as a gift. I have heard her say—though she would never go back to those dark years of her early grief—she sometimes longs for the closeness she felt to God then.

Anger blocked my intimacy with God for a long and painful time while he waited for me to bring my true heart to him. As long as I denied my anger, I put on a mask. When I got honest, his response—showing me the heaven-life of my aunt and cousin—helped me "forgive him." The wall came down between him and me.

Since God has never done anything wrong, we cannot forgive him like we forgive someone who has sinned against us. But to make peace with God we must lay down our anger, just as we do when we forgive a person. He will help us do this if we will get real. The spiritual exercises at the end of this chapter will lead you in this process.

Two Gifts and a Bracing Promise

When we suffer, our hearts cry *why?* Why did my marriage end? Why did my child die? Why did my race suffer genocide? Why did God allow this?

We are not alone in asking this—the most painful question of the human heart. Many people in the Bible cried, "Why?" Jesus himself cried out, moments before his death: "My God, my God, why have you forsaken me?" (Mark 15:34).

No one in the Bible gets an answer to this question. Maybe the answers exceed our capacity to understand. But the longer I sit with Jesus's terrible words, the more I sense the mysterious, unyielding joy of two gifts from God resounding under their despair.

The trajectory of Jesus's incarnation leads him down through every form of human suffering. He moves down from heaven's glory to the shameful poverty of childbirth in a barn, down from blinding beauty into a human body Isaiah tells us was not good looking. His life leads him down through political oppression, down through misinterpretation, rejection, betrayal, and abandonment, down through false accusations, arrest, and torture. Down, down, down, to this—the most excruciating moment—the agony of feeling abandoned by God.

Because of this trajectory, and because of this moment in particular, no matter the depth of our suffering, we have the gift of knowing we are not alone. Jesus shares our pain. He is Emmanuel, God with us, down to the last drop of agony life can wring from us. And his solidarity with us in suffering did not stop with his crucifixion. We get his Holy Spirit, with us EVERY moment: "I am with you always, to the end of the age" (Matthew 28:20).

Jesus's last words offer us another gift, a gift that shines bright hope into our despair: Jesus *felt* forsaken, but he *was not* forsaken. How do we know? Three days later, Jesus rose. Though Jesus felt forsaken in that hour, God's good purposes for Jesus were not threatened for a moment. Joy awaited Jesus (Hebrews 12:2). One day he would see what his death had accomplished and be more than satisfied (Isaiah 53:11). God was working in the dark.

Because Jesus uttered those words and then rose, his pain-filled question gives us the gift of hope. If we belong to God, nothing—not death, illness, genocide, famine, war, divorce, abuse, rejection—nothing we experience can mean God has abandoned us. From Jesus we learn our cry, "Why have you forsaken me?" though we utter it with our dying breath, is not the last word. No matter how bad it gets, God is not finished writing a story for us that will have the best ending: heaven and endless joy-filled life lie ahead.

From the perspective of heaven, our agonies—no matter

how great—are "momentary" (2 Corinthians 4:17). We will join Jesus where "death shall be no more, neither shall there be mourning, nor crying, nor pain anymore" (Revelation 21:4).

So we get two gifts: the gift of Jesus's solidarity with us in our pain and the gift of hope. We also get a bracing promise: God will come to judge the earth:

> *The day of Lord will come like a thief, and then the heavens will pass away with a roar, and the heavenly bodies will be burned up and dissolved, and the earth and the works that are done on it will be exposed...according to his promise we are waiting for new heavens and a new earth in which righteousness dwells (2 Peter 3:10, 13).*

Hebrews 2:8 says "at present we do not yet see everything in subjection to him." Though God remains ultimately in control, things here on earth are not the way he wants them. One day he will end the present structures of life. He will expose and destroy all that hurts us, and he will bring everything into subjection to himself. When that happens, "They shall not hurt or destroy in all my holy mountain; for the earth shall be full of the knowledge of the Lord as the waters cover the sea" (Isaiah 11:9).

God's coming judgement affirms our inner revulsion over genocide, sex trafficking, famine, disease, and tragic death. We are *right*. In fact, our puny rage cannot compare to what God will one day pour out on this place. I find this a bracing comfort.

So we don't get answers. We get affirmation of our inner revolt. We get him with us now—loving us. And in the end we get him face-to-face forever in a place where all suffering will end.

And he wants to know, "Are we okay, you and me?"

Spiritual Exercises for Chapter Eleven

Making Peace with God

Working through your anger at God may be a process more than a one-time event. Please consider these spiritual exercises as a map of possible steps toward full reconciliation between God's heart and yours. You may return to these steps numerous times during a season of your life, or you may find your own steps. Only please don't give up until you are certain the stone of anger at God has been torn down in your heart. May the Lord bless you and restore your soul.

Am I Angry with God?

1. Pray these words from Psalm 26: "Test me, Lord, and try me, examine my heart and my mind" (Verse 2). Ask the Lord to help you to see if you hold any anger toward him in your heart.

2. Please prayerfully read through and consider this list of potentially painful questions. They are designed to uncover hidden anger with God. I pray you can be courageous to allow your true heart to speak, but you do not need to push yourself. If you need to stop with one and wait for a while before you come back, that is okay. Only please don't avoid these questions forever.

   - When have you been disappointed with God?

   - When have you felt God did not answer your prayers?

   - What have been the most traumatic moments of your life?

   - Are you "okay" with God about these moments?

3. Journal anything that is on your heart.

Bringing Your True Heart to God

1. If you do have anger toward God in your heart, you are not alone. Many of God's people expressed anger and perplexity in their prayers. Do you identify with any of these expressions:

   - Psalm 22:1: "My God, my God, why have you forsaken me? Why are you so far from saving me, from the words of my groaning?"

   - Job 30:19: "God has cast me into the mire, and I have become like dust and ashes."

   - Jeremiah 15:17-18: "I did not sit in the company of revelers, nor did I rejoice; I sat alone, because your hand was upon me, for you had filled me with indignation. Why is my pain unceasing, my wound incurable, refusing to be healed? Will you be to me like a deceitful brook, like waters that fail?"

   - Psalm 89:49: "Lord, where is your steadfast love of old?"

   - John 11:21: "Lord, if you had been here, my brother would not have died." (*You may substitute any statement from your heart for "my brother would not have died."*)

   - Jonah 4:9: "I do well to be angry, angry enough to die."

2. In an attitude of prayer and confession, beginning with the verse you have chosen or another that comes to mind, tell God what is truly in your heart toward him. What do you blame him for? What makes it hard for you to trust him?

3. Take time to experience any emotions of grief or fear that are connected with the anger you feel.

4. Ask God to help you with these feelings. Ask him if there is

anything he would like to say to you or show you. Journal any thoughts, impressions, pictures, or words that come to your mind.

Clarifying Promises

Sometimes our anger at God comes from our sense of injustice. Like Job, we feel we have done everything right and our suffering is therefore unjust. We feel God has not kept up his end of the bargain. We may be helped by recalling what God has promised and what he has not.

1. Prayerfully read the following verses, considering what God says about suffering and trouble:

   • Job 5:7: "Man is born to trouble as the sparks fly upward."

   • John 16:33: "In the world you will have tribulation. But take heart; I have overcome the world."

   • Psalm 94:19: "When the cares of my heart are many, your consolations cheer my soul."

   • Psalm 34:19: "Many are the afflictions of the righteous, but the Lord delivers him out of them all."

   • Isaiah 53:3: "He was despised and rejected by men; a man of sorrows, and acquainted with grief."

   • John 15:18: "If the world hates you, know that it has hated me before it hated you."

2. Prayerfully read the following verses, considering what God says about comfort and hope:

   • Psalm 23:4: "Even though I walk through the valley of the shadow of death, I will fear no evil, for you are with me."

- Matthew 28:20: "I am with you always, to the end of the age."

- Hebrews 13:5: "I will never leave you nor forsake you."

- 2 Corinthians 1:3-4: "Blessed be the God and Father of our Lord Jesus Christ, the Father of mercies and God of all comfort, who comforts us in all our affliction."

- 2 Corinthians 4:17: "For this light momentary affliction is preparing for us an eternal weight of glory beyond all comparison."

- Isaiah 63:9: "In all their affliction he was afflicted."

- Isaiah 53:4-5: "Surely he has borne our griefs and carried our sorrows; yet we esteemed him stricken, smitten by God, and afflicted. But he was pierced for our transgressions; he was crushed for our iniquities; upon him was the chastisement that brought us peace, and with his wounds we are healed."

- John 11:35: "Jesus wept."

- Revelation 21:4: "He will wipe away every tear from their eyes, and death shall be no more, neither shall there be mourning, nor crying, nor pain anymore, for the former things have passed away."

3. Write down what you see in both collections of verses. What is the Lord speaking to you about these things? Have you had false expectations of God?

4. Tell the Lord what is on your heart in regards to these things and listen for what he might say to you or show you.

Repentance

1. A.W. Tozer writes, "What comes into our minds when we think about God is the most important thing about us."[32] If we have been angry with God, somewhere along the line our thinking about him has gotten skewed, because, regardless of our feelings, God *is* good.

2. Prayerfully read Isaiah 53:4-5: "Surely he has borne our griefs and carried our sorrows; yet we esteemed him stricken, smitten by God, and afflicted. But he was pierced for our transgressions; he was crushed for our iniquities; upon him was the chastisement that brought us peace, and with his wounds we are healed."

3. Take time to tell God, in an attitude of repentance, the negative thoughts you have had toward him.

4. When you can, make Job 42:3 part of your confession: "Surely I spoke of things I did not understand, things too wonderful for me to know" (NIV).

5. Picture, if you can, the Lord on the cross and yourself at his feet. Ask him to help you think true thoughts about him, to help you believe in his love, mercy, and goodness in spite of how bad things can seem down here. Ask him to forgive you for thinking badly of him and to give you his Holy Spirit to help you lay down your anger and to love him.

Discussion Questions for Chapter Eleven:
The Stone of Anger at God

1. What has been your experience with hearing people say "I cannot believe in a God who would_____"?

2. What, if anything, has been your response to such statements?

3. Do you know someone who is openly angry at God? Why are they angry and what has been the result in their life, as far as you can see, of this anger?

4. Describe any difficulties you have had believing that God loves you. If this is not difficult for you, please talk about how you experience God's love or what knowing he loves you means for you.

5. What are your thoughts about the possibility that people may need to "forgive" God?

6. Describe any experiences you have had in expressing difficult emotions to God. What happened?

7. What comfort in suffering do you find from the hope of heaven and the certainty of judgment?

8. What comfort in suffering do you find in the life, death, and resurrection of Jesus?

9. Did you discover any anger at God in your heart as you worked through the spiritual exercises? Please explain.

10. Were you able, through the exercises, to make peace with God? What was that experience like?

Chapter Twelve
What I Hope for You

"I have loved you with an everlasting love."
~ Jeremiah 31:3

I wrote *Stone by Stone* to give you hope and courage to fight through anything preventing you from knowing God more deeply. He gave me a glimpse of his heart, and I found the love in it sweeter, more joyous, and better than anything I ever imagined.

And my experience of his love is not unique.

The Writers of Scripture Exalt in Being Loved by God

- David says to God, "Your steadfast love is better than life" (Psalm 63:3).

- Paul describes Jesus as "The Son of God, who loved me and gave himself for me" (Galatians 2:20) and says, "God's love has been poured into our hearts through the Holy Spirit" (Romans 5:5).

- John calls himself the "disciple whom Jesus loved" (John 21:7) and says, "we have come *to know* and *to believe* the love that God has for us" (1 John 4:16, emphasis added).

- And Paul prays for every Christian to know the immensity of God's love for them: "that you, being rooted and grounded in love, may have strength to comprehend with all the saints what is the breadth and length and height and depth, and to know the love of Christ that surpasses knowledge, that you may be filled with all the fullness of God" (Ephesians 3:17-19).

Christian Writers Celebrate God's Love for Them

- Julian of Norwich: "For we are so preciously loved by God that we cannot even comprehend it. No created being can ever know how much and how sweetly and tenderly God loves them."

- Charles Finney: "Indeed, it seemed to come in waves and waves of liquid love.... No words can express the wonderful love that was shed abroad in my heart. I wept aloud with joy and love."[33]

- A. W. Tozer: "The love of God is one of the great realities of the universe, a pillar upon which the hope of the world rests. But it is a personal, intimate thing, too. God does not love populations, He loves people. He loves not masses, but men. He loves us all with a mighty love that has no beginning and can have no end.... True Christian joy is the heart's harmonious response to the Lord's song of love."[34]

Our Hymns Strain for Words Powerful Enough to Express this Love

- O the deep, deep love of Jesus, vast, unmeasured, boundless, free!
Rolling as a mighty ocean in its fullness over me!

Underneath me, all around me, is the current of Thy love.[35]

- Could we with ink the ocean fill,
  And were the skies of parchment made,
  Were every stalk on earth a quill,
  And every man a scribe by trade,
  To write the love of God above,
  Would drain the ocean dry.[36]

- Jesus loves me, this I know
  For the Bible tells me so.

- See from His head, His hands, His feet,
  Sorrow and love flow mingled down!
  Did e'er such love and sorrow meet,
  Or thorns compose so rich a crown?

  Were the whole realm of nature mine,
  That were a present far too small;
  Love so amazing, so divine,
  Demands my soul, my life, my all.[37]

God desires for all Christians to live in the joy of knowing he loves us. He wants us to experience security, comfort, and healing in his love. The truth is, the Christian life only makes sense when we experience, know, and rely upon this love. I want this for you.

If you, like me, have had a hard time delighting in God's love, I hope I have helped you tear down any wall—stone by stone—between God's heart and yours. I earnestly hope you have found the "inexpressible and glorious joy" (1 Peter 1:8) of knowing the love God has for you. But if you still want more, please don't give up. He promises, "You will seek me and find me, when you seek me with all your heart. I will be found by you" (Jeremiah 29:13-14).

May you make space for him. May you have perseverance to wait for him. May you seek him with all of your heart until the stones come down and the warmth of his passion for you fills you with joy. He created you for this.

Bibliography

1. C.S. Lewis, *The Lion, the Witch, and the Wardrobe* (Harper-Collins, 1950), 179.

2. C.S. Lewis, *The Lion, the Witch, and the Wardrobe* (Harper-Collins, 1950), 20.

3. J.I. Packer, *Rediscovering Holiness* (Baker Books, Reissue edition, 2009), 49.

4. Leanne Payne is the author of *The Healing Presence* and *Restoring the Christian Soul Through Healing Prayer,* among other books. She also founded Pastoral Care Ministries in Wheaton, Illinois.

5. John Piper, *Finally Alive* (Christian Focus Publications Ltd., 2009), 89.

6. Leanne Payne, *Restoring the Christian Soul* (Baker Books, 1996), 143.

7. Extracts by CS Lewis © copyright CS Lewis Pte Ltd. *Prayer: Letters to Malcolm* (Collins, Fountain Books, 1977), 83.

8. David G. Benner, *The Gift of Being Yourself* (Downers Grove, IL: InterVarsity Press, 2004), 76.

9. Please refer to *Humility* by Andrew Murray (Whitaker House, 1982) for an exploration of this truth.

10. Andrew Murray, *Humility* (Whitaker House, 1982), 18, 10.

11. I am thankful for David G. Benner's outline of thoughts on

Peter in his book *The Gift of Being Yourself* (Downers Grove, IL: InterVarsity Press, 2004).

12. Alexandar Wolff and David Epstein. *Sports Illustrated* (October 22, 2012).

13. C. S. Lewis, *Mere Christianity* (HarperCollins 2001), 226.

14. A.W. Tozer, *Knowledge of the Holy*, Public Domain.

15. Extracts by CS Lewis © copyright CS Lewis Pte Ltd. *The Collected Letters of C. S. Lewis, Volume 3: Narnia, Cambridge, and Joy 1950-1963*, 123.

16. W.Kimnach, K. Minkema, D. Sweeney, eds, *The Sermons of Jonathan Edwards: A Reader* (Yale, 1999), pp. 127-128.

17. A.W. Tozer, *Knowledge of the Holy*, Public Domain.

18. A.W. Tozer, *Knowledge of the Holy*, Public Domain.

19. Martina McBride, *How I Feel* (Waking Up Laughing, RCA Records, Sbme 2007) Writer(s): Christopher Marsh Lindsey, Brad Douglas Warren, Martina McBride, Brad Warren, Brett Warren, Aimee Mayo, Brett Daniel Warren. Copyright: Delemmava Music, Emi Blackwood Music Inc., Little Blue Typewriter Music, Moonscar Music, Warner-tamerlane Publishing Corp., Stylesonic Music LLC.

20. Leanne Payne, *Restoring the Christian Soul* (Baker Books, 1996), 82.

21. Leanne Payne, *Restoring the Christian Soul* (Baker Books, 1996), 85.

22. Rebecca Jean Terry, *Help me Be a Good Girl Amen: My Journey from Missionary Kid to Truth* (CreateSpace Independent Publishing Platform, 2011), 81.

23. Rebecca Jean Terry, *Help me Be a Good Girl Amen: My Journey from Missionary Kid to Truth* (CreateSpace Independent Publishing Platform, 2011), 83-84.

24. Leanne Payne, *Restoring the Christian Soul* (Baker Books, 1996), 39.

25. Charles H. Kraft, *Deep Wounds, Deep Healing* (Chosen Books, Revised edition, 2010), 17.

26. Charles H. Kraft, *Deep Wounds, Deep Healing* (Chosen Books, Revised edition, 2010), 29.

27. Leanne Payne, *Restoring the Christian Soul* (Baker Books, 1996), 39.

28. Leanne Payne, *The Healing Presence* (Baker Books, 1995), 164.

29. I first learned of these different types of demonic spirits from Francis MacNutt's book *Deliverance from Evil Spirits* (Chosen Books, 1995).

30. I was introduced to the practice of creating such a family tree through the ministry of Christian Healing Ministries, Inc. For a more a detailed explanation, please see their "Personal Information Form."

31. Charles H. Kraft, *Deep Wounds, Deep Healing* (Chosen Books, Revised edition, 2010), 193-4.

32. A.W. Tozer, *Knowledge of the Holy*, Public Domain.

33. A.M. Hills, *The Life of Charles G. Finney*, Public Domain.

34. A. W. Tozer, *Knowledge of the Holy*, Public Domain.

35. Samuel Francis, "O the Deep, Deep Love of Jesus," (1875),

Music by Thomas Williams (1890).

36. Frederick M. Lehman, "The Love of God" (1917), arranged by his daughter, Claudia L. Mays.

37. Isaac Watts, "When I Survey the Wondrous Cross" (1707), Music by Lowell Mason.

Acknowledgments

To write a book is to depend deeply on a supportive and generous community. I thank my husband, Doug, for loving me through so many of my steps toward healing and for believing unfailingly in Stone by Stone. I thank my children, Hannah, Audrey, and Jonathan, for filling my heart to bursting with joy and love. I thank my mom, Grace Lukens, and my sister, Heather Schmitt, for reading and cheering me on. I thank my dad, Bob Dolan, for believing in me without limit. I thank Lisa Hoyer, who read and re-read so many chapters and encouraged me time and again. I thank Brad Long, Cindy Strickler, Eugene Peterson, Kathleen Christopher, Kay Morrison, Linda Williams, and Tom Ashbrook, for taking time to endorse this book. I thank Annie Sears, Betty Brown, Jill Bachali, Michelle Koenig, and Sarah Harrison for proof-reading the manuscript. I thank Dina Sleiman, Roseanna White, and Wendy Chorot at WhiteFire for choosing to publish Stone by Stone and for being the kindest, most friendly editors and publishers imaginable. And I thank the long-time members of the Intensive Healing Prayer at Cornerstone Community Church, whose passion to seek Jesus for healing, deep love for the hurting, and abiding humility incubated me as I learned to pray for others: Dave Ottem, Karen Wittnam, Lyn and Phyllis Robinson, Sidney Graff, and Terry Matthews. I will always treasure the hours we spent in prayer together.

JASONA BROWN grew up on the Washington coast (think rain, coffee, and wool socks with Birkenstocks) and spent her summers on a fishing boat in Alaska (think more rain, fish slime, and leaping humpback whales). In *Stone by Stone* she tells the story of the healing of her relationship with God. Childhood trauma—a life-threatening head injury, eight years of constant helmet-wearing, and the murders of her aunt and young cousin—caused Jasona to build a wall between God's heart and hers. Decades later, God helped her tear it down, and she came alive to the love in his heart. She writes from a longing to invite readers to experience and rely upon God's love for them. Jasona holds a Master's Degree in Christian Studies from Regent College. She lives in Colorado with her husband and three children.

CPSIA information can be obtained
at www.ICGtesting.com
Printed in the USA
FSOW01n0754120915
10938FS